dabblelab

Manga Drawing with

DC

# HOW TO DRAW SUPERMAN™ MANGA!

by Christopher Harbo

illustrated by Haining

Superman created by Jerry Siegel and Joe Shuster
by special arrangement with the Jerry Siegel family

CAPSTONE PRESS
a capstone imprint

Published by Capstone Press, an imprint of Capstone.
1710 Roe Crest Drive
North Mankato, Minnesota 56003
capstonepub.com

Copyright © 2023 DC.
SUPERMAN and all related characters and elements © & ™ DC. (s23)

All rights reserved. No part of this publication may be reproduced in whole or in part, or stored in a retrieval system, or transmitted in any form or by any means, electronic, mechanical, photocopying, recording, or otherwise, without written permission of the publisher.

Library of Congress Cataloging-in-Publication Data
is available on the Library of Congress website.
ISBN: 9781669021681 (hardcover)
ISBN: 9781669021643 (ebook PDF)

Summary: Superman and manga unite! Put a new spin on iconic Metropolis Super Heroes and Super-Villains and learn how to draw them as dynamic manga characters with easy-to-follow steps.

Editorial Credits
Editor: Abby Huff; Designer: Hilary Wacholz;
Media Researcher: Jo Miller; Production Specialist: Tori Abraham

Image Credits
Photos: Capstone Studio: Karon Dubke 5 (all), Backgrounds and design elements: Capstone

The publisher and the author shall not be liable for any damages allegedly arising from the information in this book, and they specifically disclaim any liability from the use or application of any of the contents of this book.

Printed in the United States     5892

# TABLE OF CONTENTS

SOAR INTO MANGA! . . . . . . . . . 4

THE MANGAKA'S TOOLKIT . . . . . . . 5

SUPERMAN . . . . . . . . . . . . 6

SUPERGIRL . . . . . . . . . . . . 8

LOIS LANE . . . . . . . . . . . . 10

JIMMY OLSEN . . . . . . . . . . . 12

POWER GIRL . . . . . . . . . . . 14

LEX LUTHOR . . . . . . . . . . . 16

BIZARRO . . . . . . . . . . . . . 18

DARKSEID . . . . . . . . . . . . 20

LIVEWIRE . . . . . . . . . . . . 22

BRAINIAC . . . . . . . . . . . . 24

LOBO . . . . . . . . . . . . . . 26

SUPERMAN VS. DOOMSDAY . . . . . . 28

MORE MANGA DRAWING FUN! . . . . . . 32

MORE DC SUPER HERO FUN! . . . . . . 32

# SOAR INTO MANGA!

Superman's origins run deep. The iconic Super Hero has been a beacon of truth and justice for the city of Metropolis since 1938! Over the years, his adventures have leaped from the pages of comic books to TV and movie screens. But that's not all! The Man of Steel also soared into Japanese comics. In 1959, *Superman* by Tatsuo Yoshida featured The World's Greatest Hero in manga!

The origin of Japanese comics and graphic novels may be just as amazing as the heroic Kryptonian's. Believe it or not, the manga art style can be traced back more than 800 years! In that time, manga has grown and evolved into one of the most popular art forms on the planet. What makes manga shine? Perhaps it's the cool characters with large eyes, small noses and mouths, and pointed chins. Or maybe it's the eye-popping art and jaw-dropping action. Either way, these comics never hold back when it comes to reeling in readers!

**SO DON'T HOLD BACK A MOMENT MORE! IT'S TIME TO SOAR BY REUNITING SUPERMAN WITH MANGA. DRAW METROPOLIS SUPER HEROES AND SUPER-VILLAINS IN MANGA STYLE!**

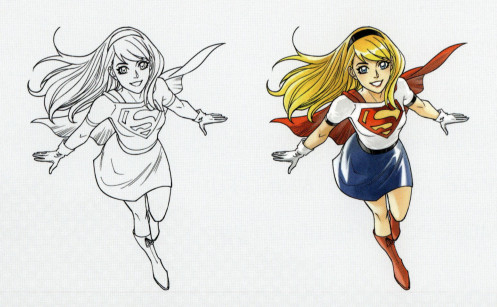

# THE MANGAKA'S TOOLKIT

All manga artists—or mangaka—need the right tools to make amazing art. Gather the following supplies before you begin drawing:

## PAPER

Art supply and hobby stores have many types of special drawing paper. But any blank, unlined paper will work well too.

## PENCILS

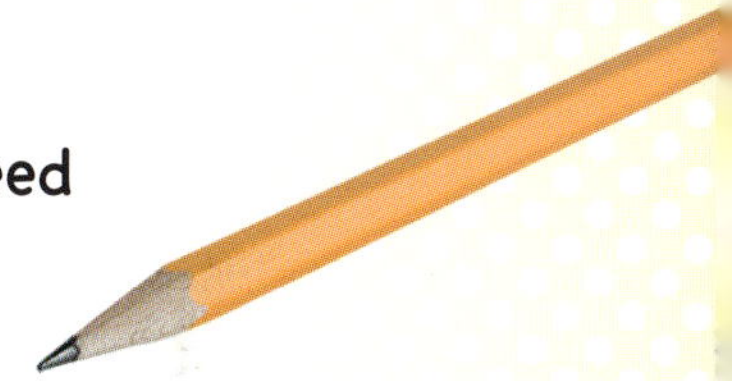

Sketch in pencil first. That way, if you make a mistake or need to change a detail, it's easy to erase and redraw.

## PENCIL SHARPENER

Keep a good pencil sharpener within reach. Sharp pencils will help you draw clean lines.

## ERASERS

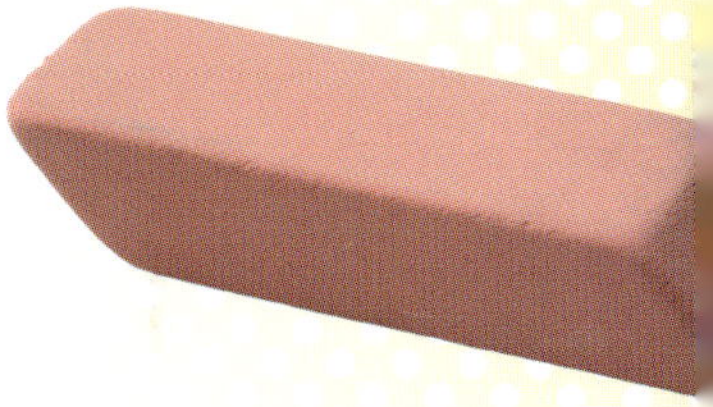

Making mistakes is a normal part of drawing. Regular pencil erasers work in a pinch. But high-quality rubber or kneaded erasers last longer and won't damage your paper.

## BLACK MARKER PENS

When your sketch is done, trace over the final lines with a black marker pen. By "inking" the lines, your characters will practically leap off the page!

## COLORED PENCILS AND MARKERS

While manga stories are usually created in black and white, they often have full-color covers. Feel free to complete your manga masterpiece with colored pencils and markers. There's nothing like a pop of color to bring characters to life!

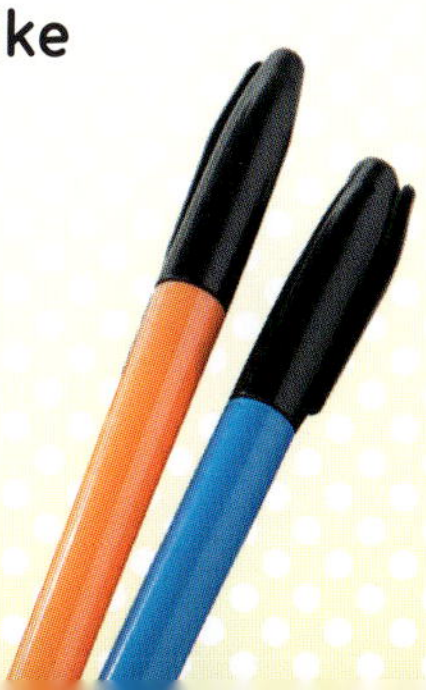

# SUPERMAN

Supercharged by Earth's yellow sun, Superman is packed with powers. Super-strength? Check. Super-breath and super-hearing? Double check. Heat vision, X-ray vision, and flight? Triple check! But what is the Man of Steel's greatest strength? His solemn promise to use his might for all that is good and right!

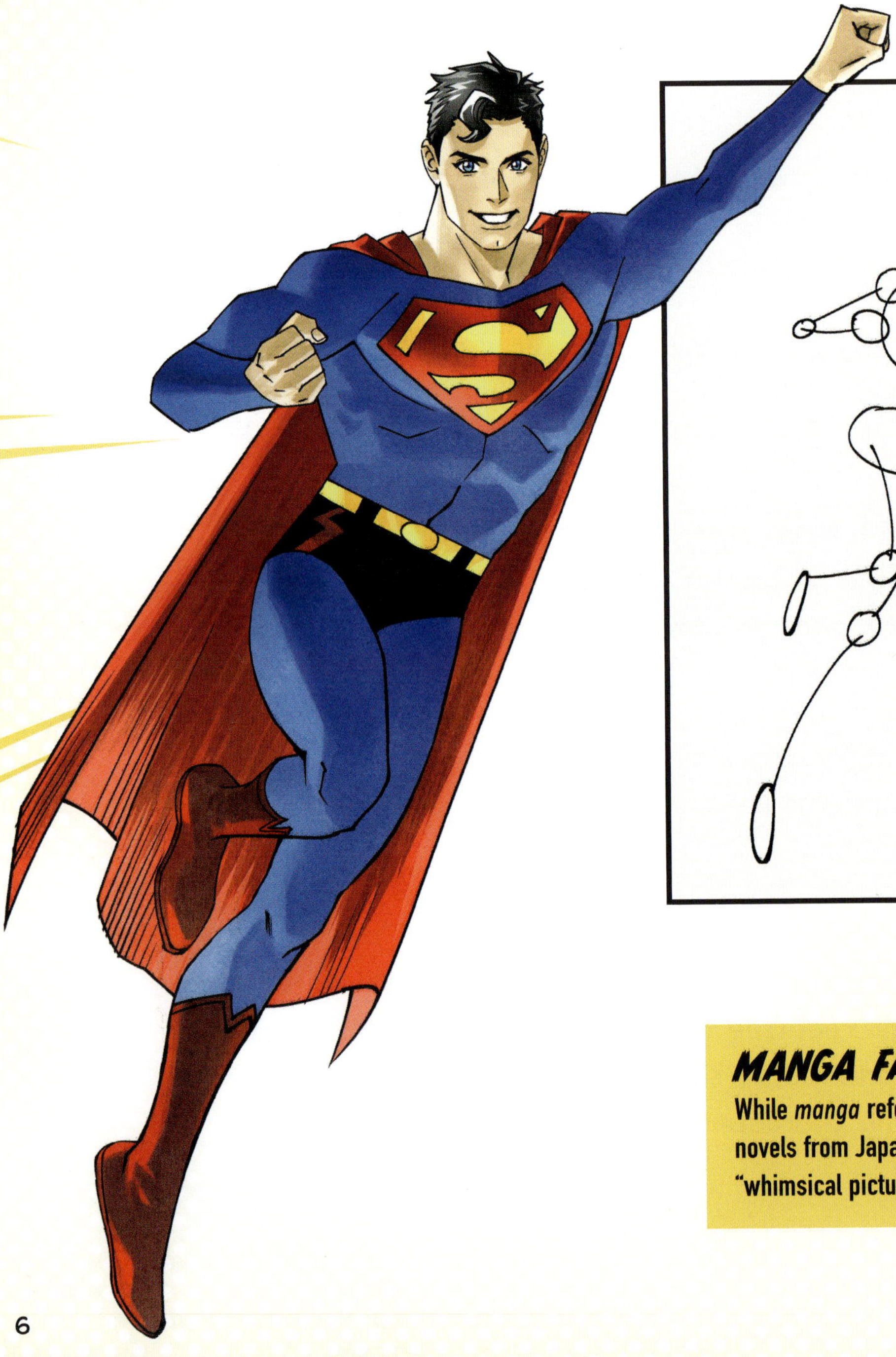

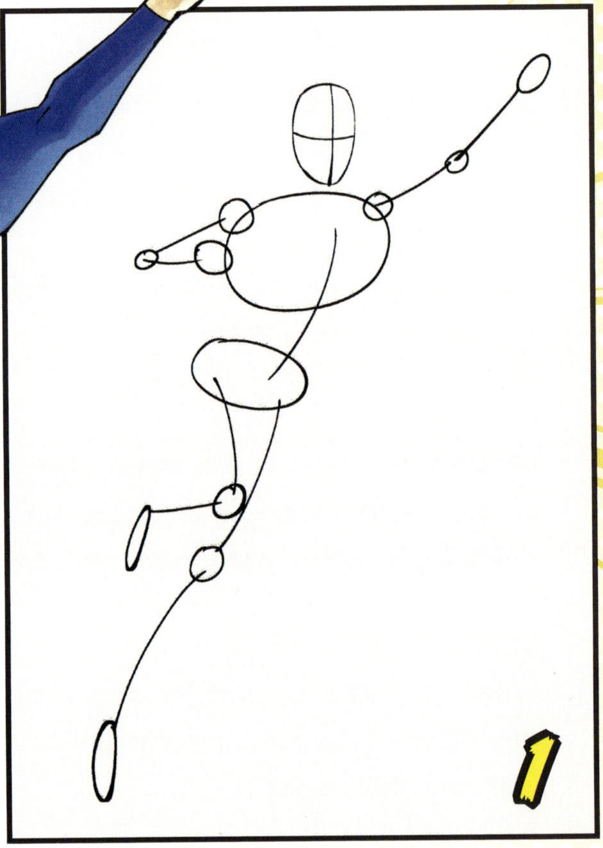
1

### MANGA FACT

While *manga* refers to comics and graphic novels from Japan, the word itself means "whimsical pictures" in Japanese.

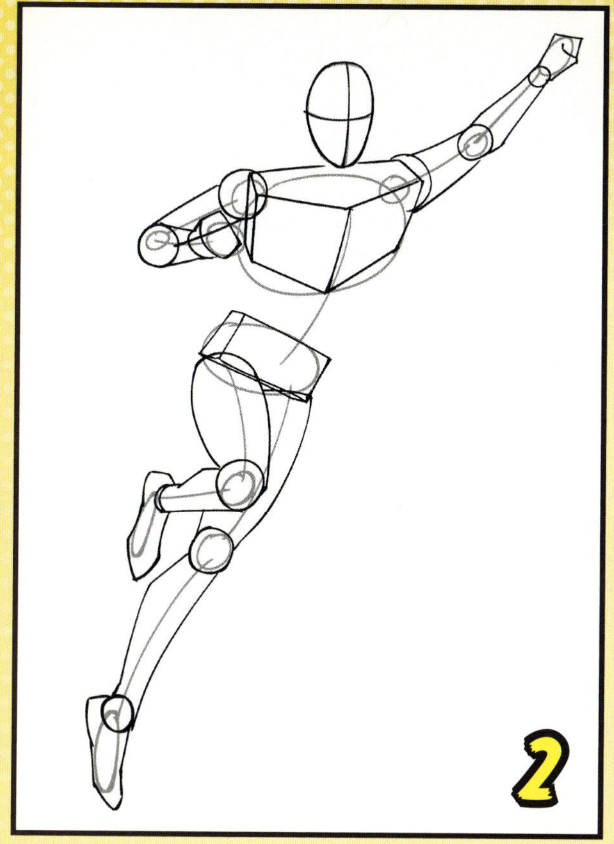
2

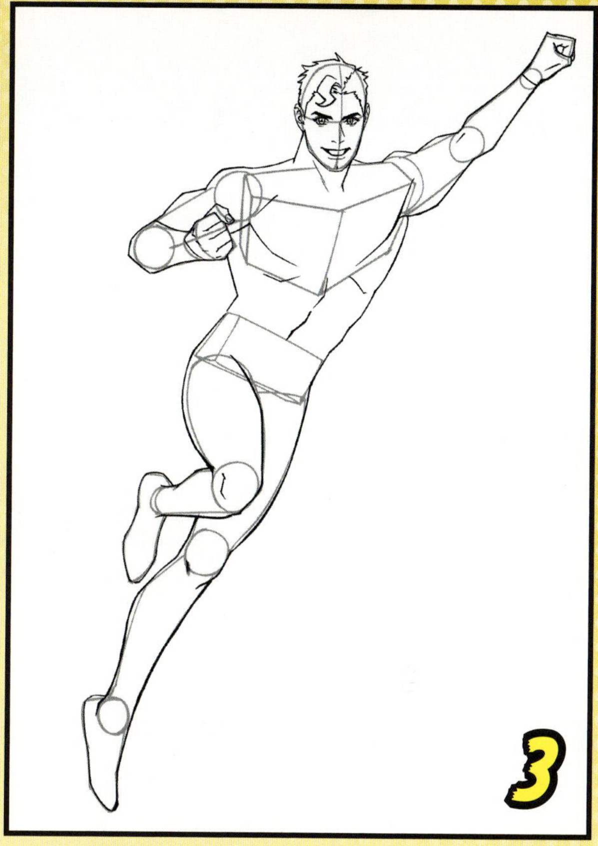
3

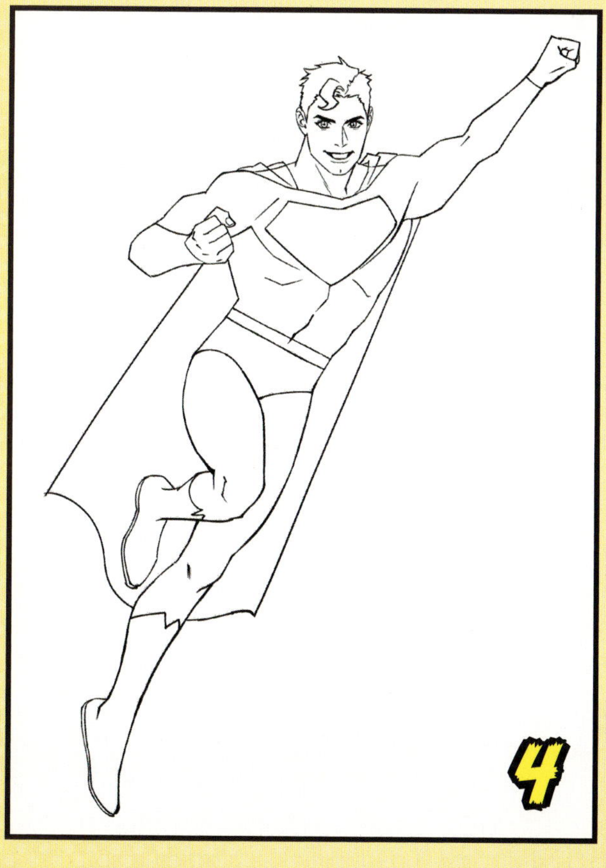
4

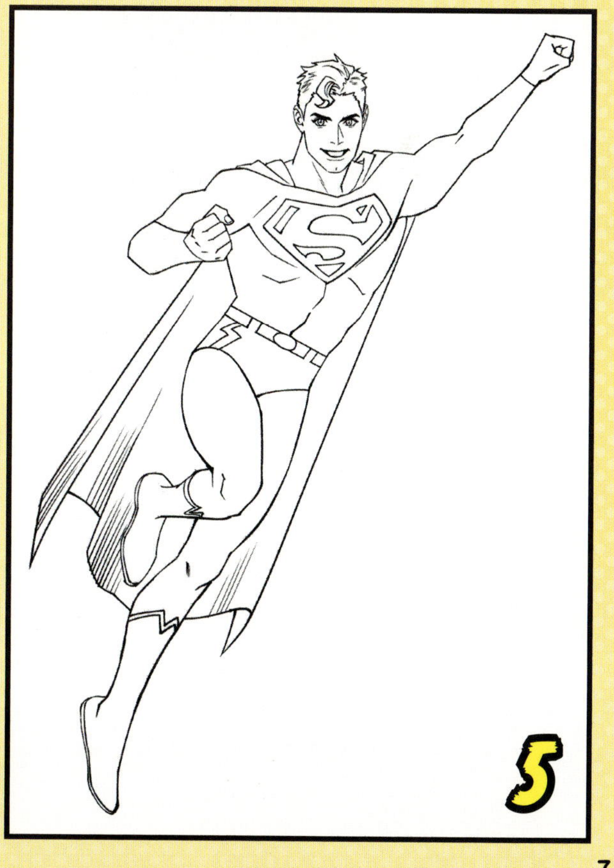
5

# SUPERGIRL

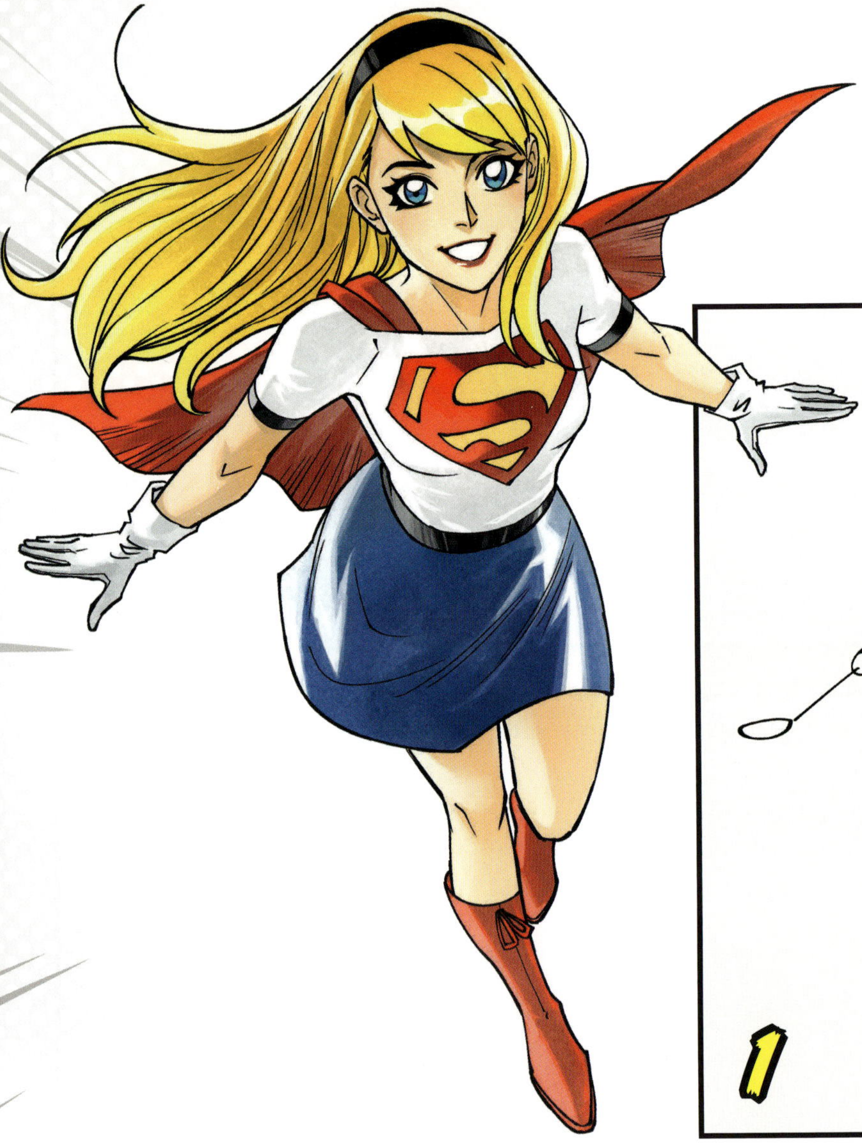

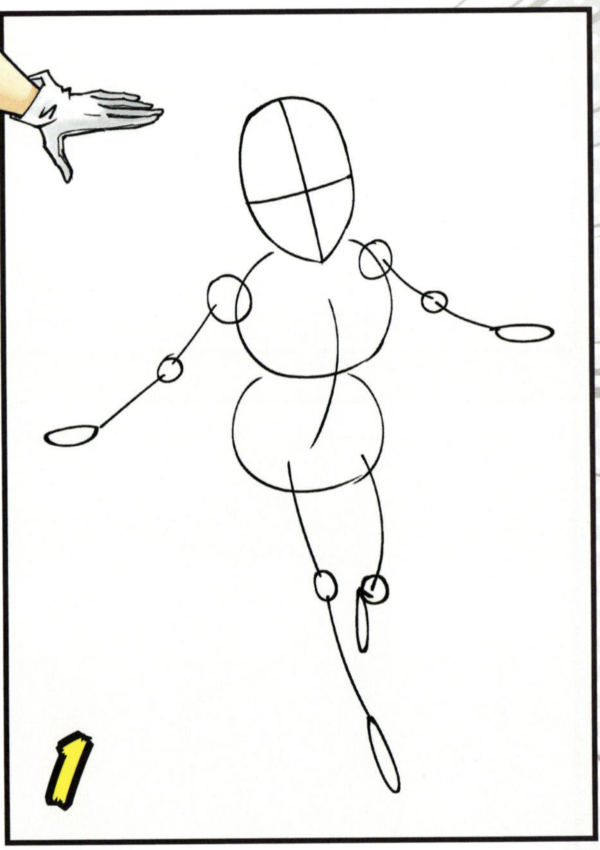
1

Supergirl is a hero with a heart of gold. Like her cousin, Superman, she can bend steel beams with her bare hands and blow out blazes with freeze-breath blasts. Most importantly, the teen shares her cousin's pledge to act with kindness and courage. The Girl of Steel will zoom to the ends of the Earth to protect people in peril!

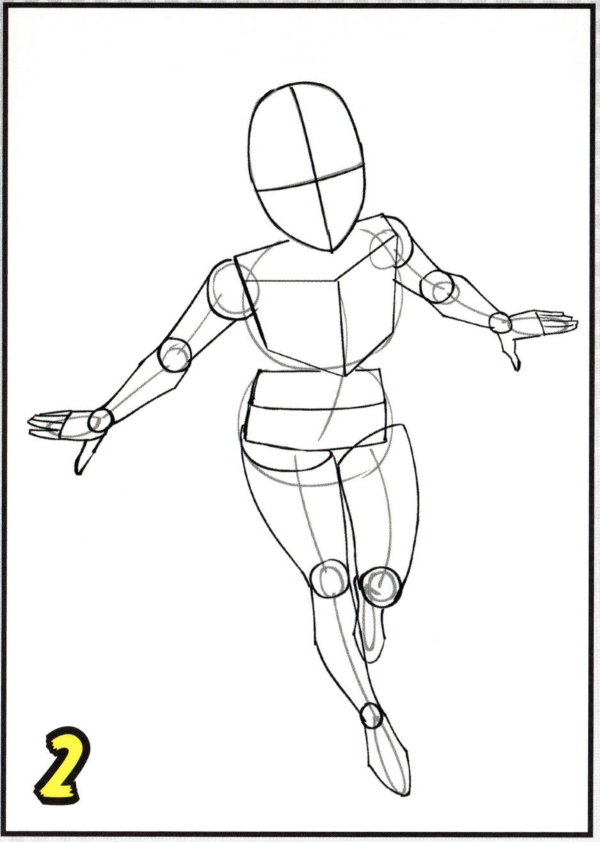
2

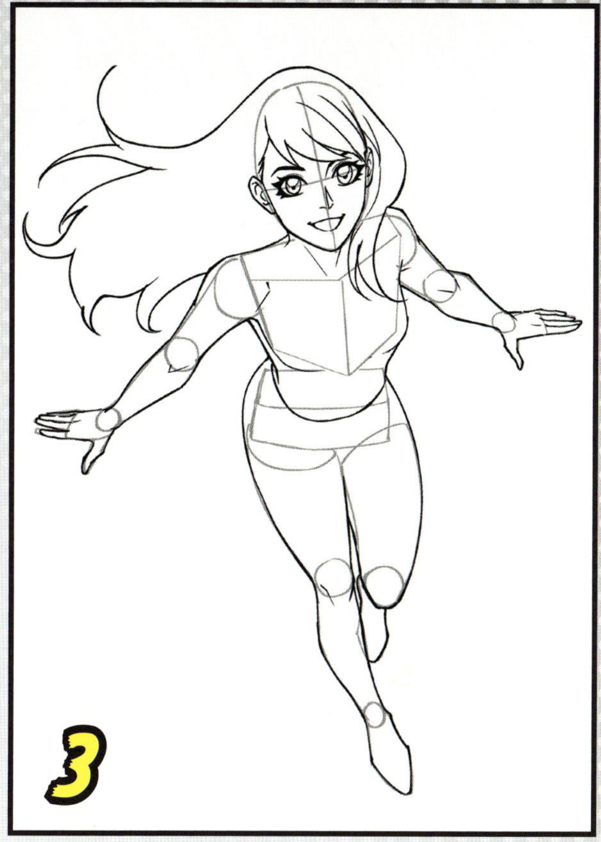
3

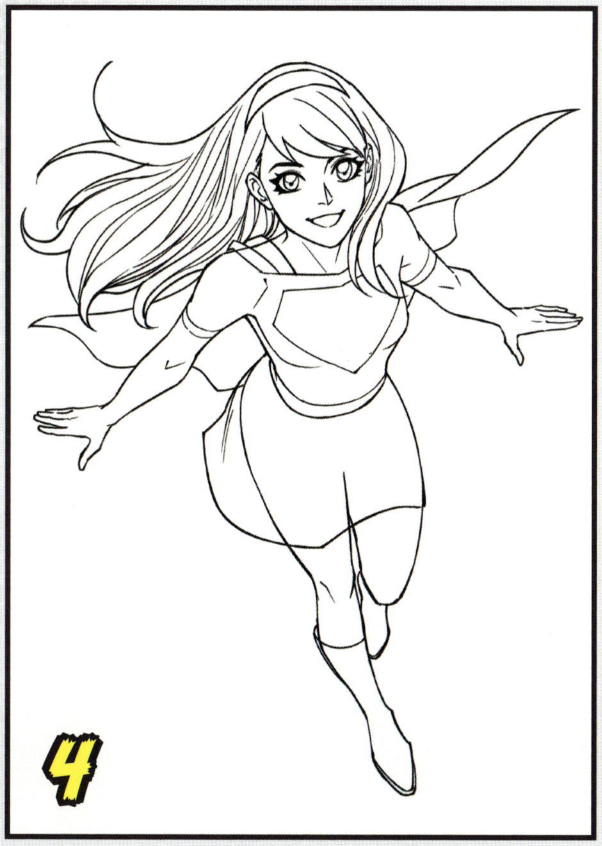
4

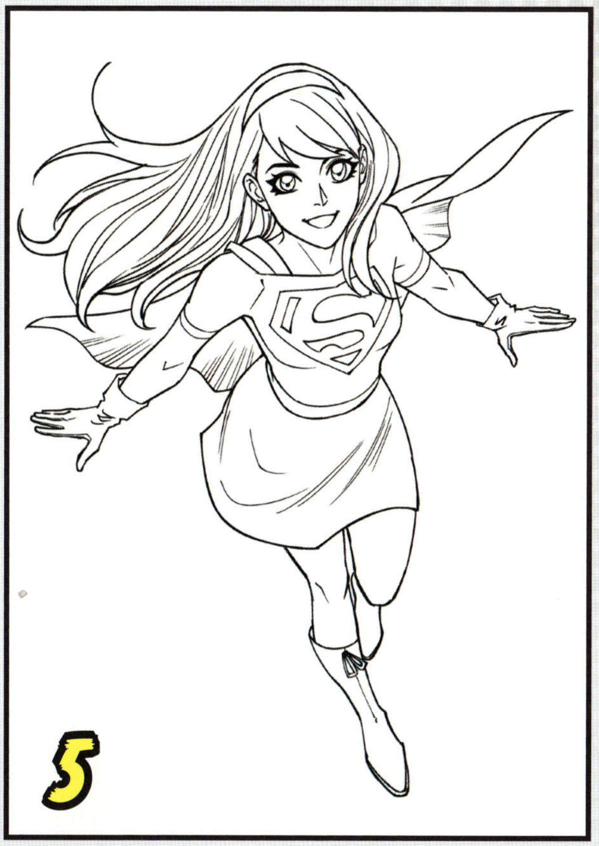
5

# LOIS LANE

Lois Lane is always on the hunt for a headline. The star reporter for the *Daily Planet* has a knack for rooting out rogues with her unique brand of journalistic justice. But if Superman happens to swoop overhead, hang on tight! Lois will dash into danger on a dime to nab her next big scoop!

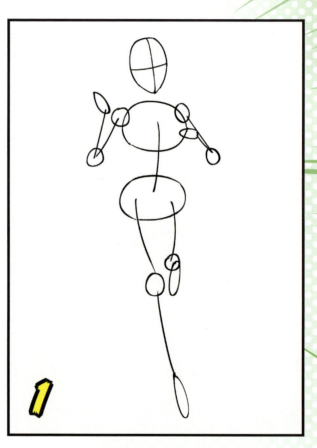

1

### MANGA FACT
Manga is read right to left because Japanese is read that way. Each page starts at the top right corner, then moves panel by panel to end at the bottom left corner.

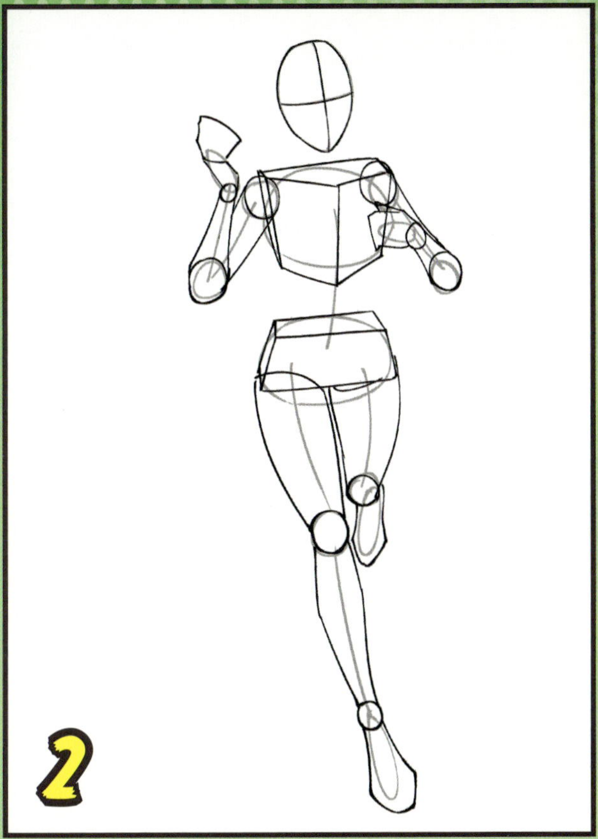
2
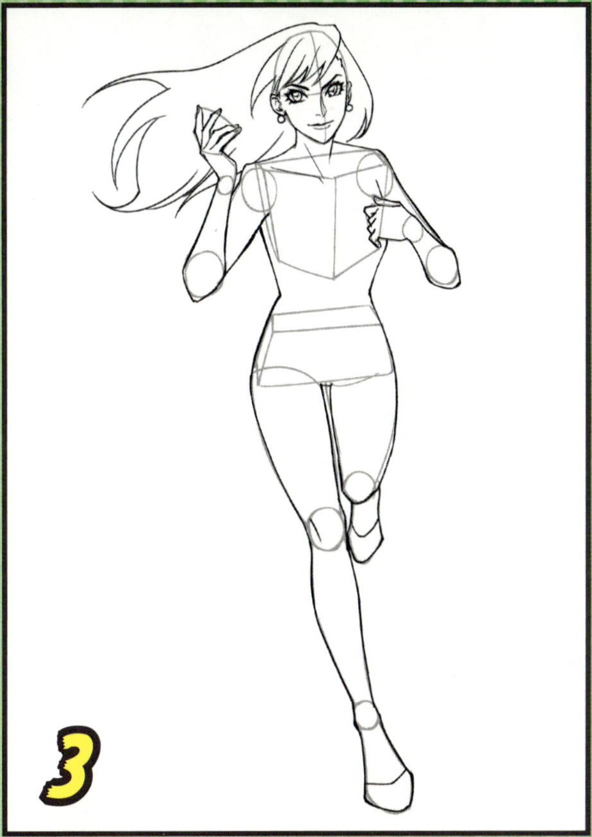
3
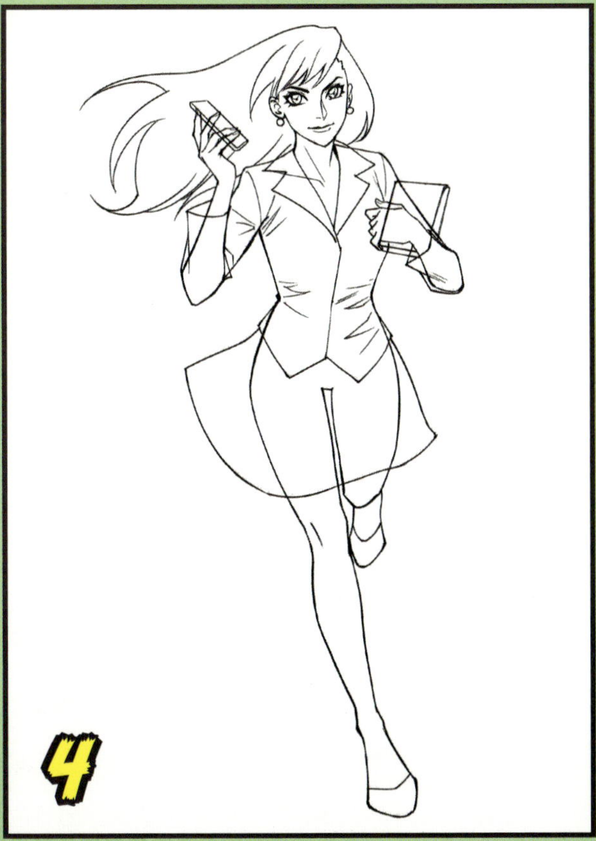
4
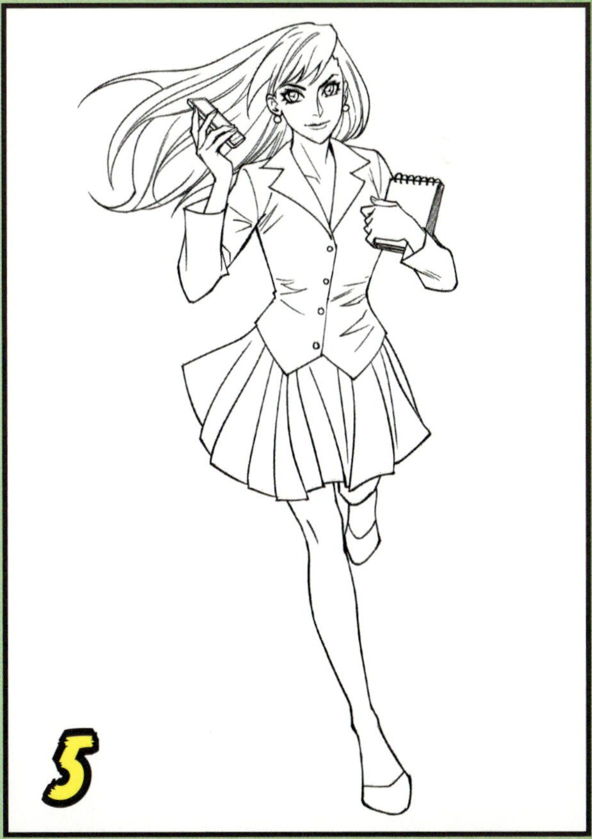
5

# JIMMY OLSEN

If a picture is worth a thousand words, then Jimmy Olsen may be one of the world's greatest storytellers. The *Daily Planet* photographer has captured hundreds of amazing moments—including many of the Man of Steel's greatest feats. Whenever Lois needs snapshots for her news stories, Jimmy's pics do the trick!

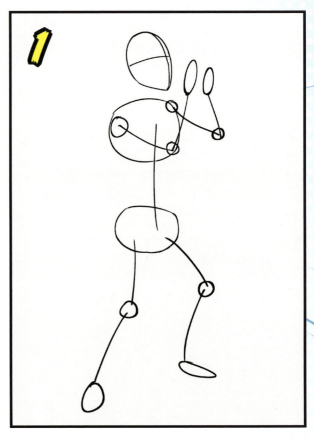

### MANGA FACT
Manga characters may be stylized, but most are based on real human anatomy. Study pictures of people to help get your characters' proportions just right.

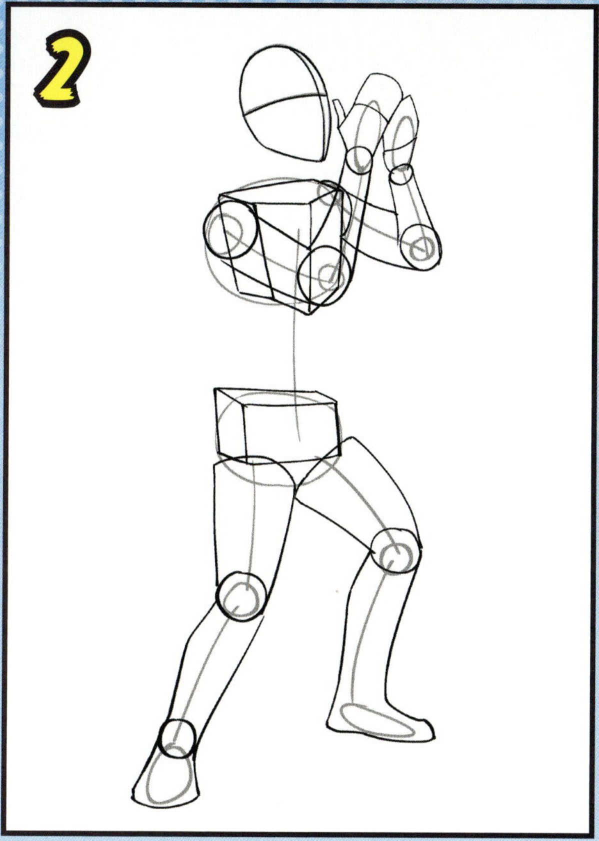
2

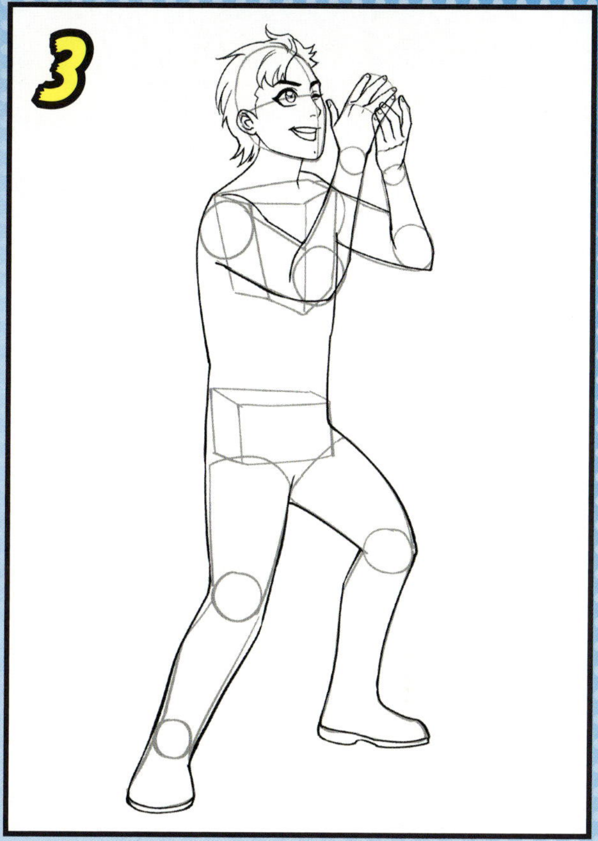
3

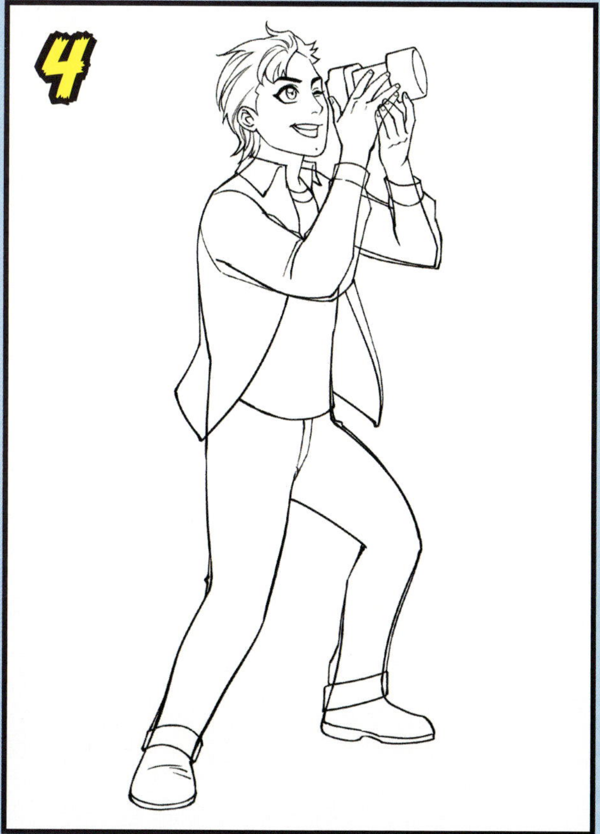
4

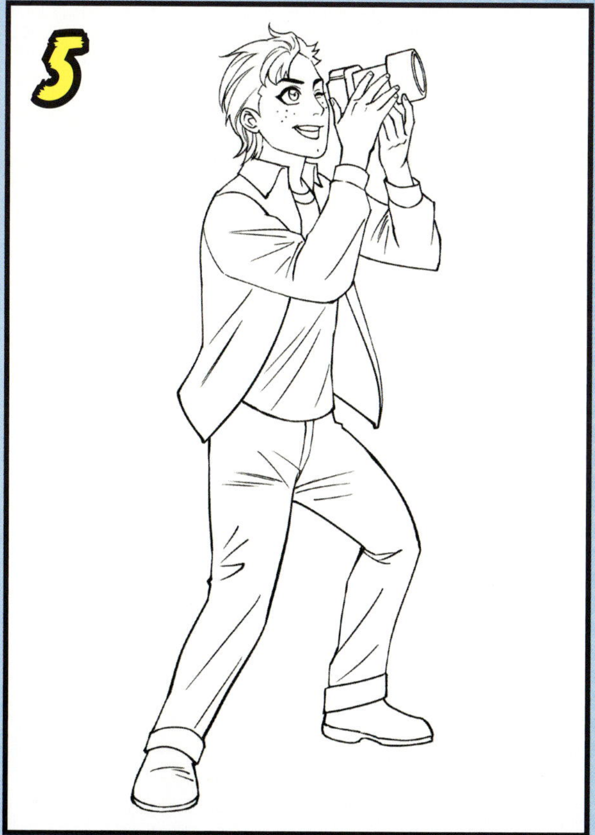
5

# POWER GIRL

Behold Power Girl as she descends to defend the defenseless! She may be Supergirl's double from an alternate universe, but this Super Hero has a style that's all her own. With amazing Kryptonian abilities, expert boxing skills, and a whip-smart mind, Power Girl quickly takes any criminal to the cleaners!

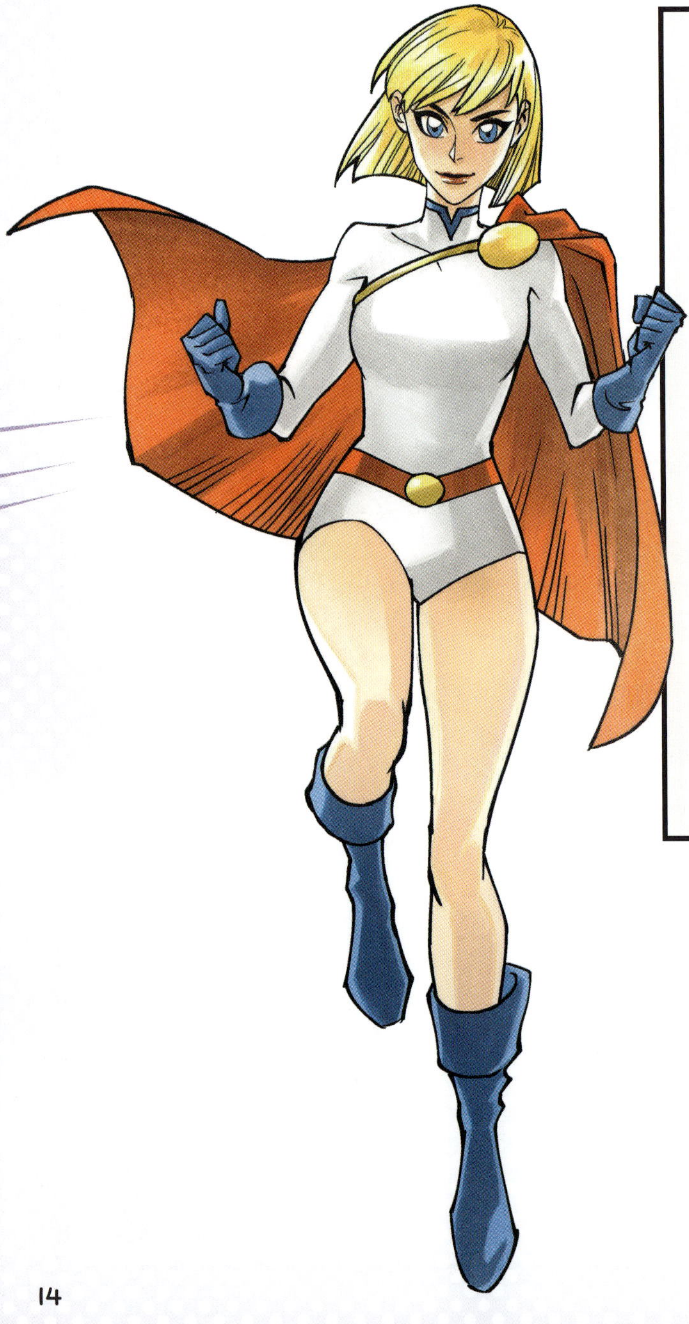

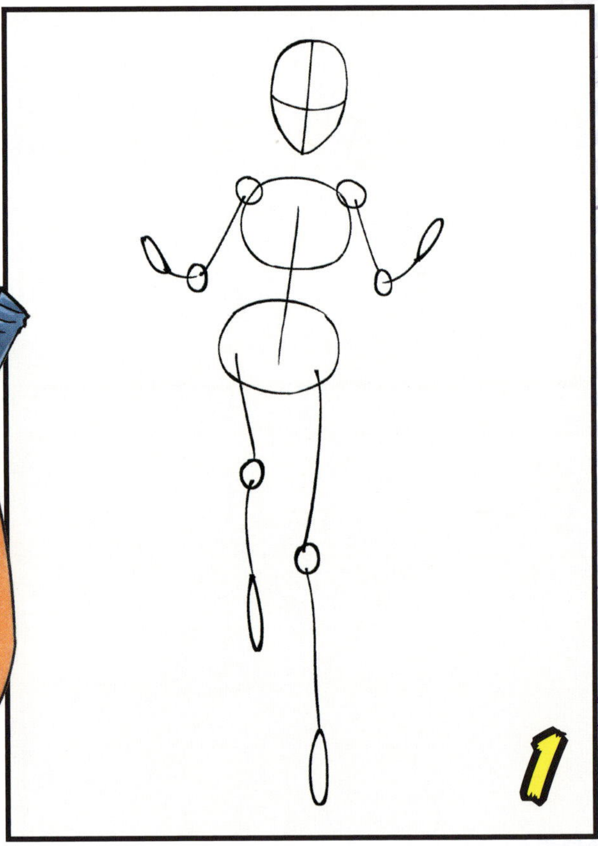
1

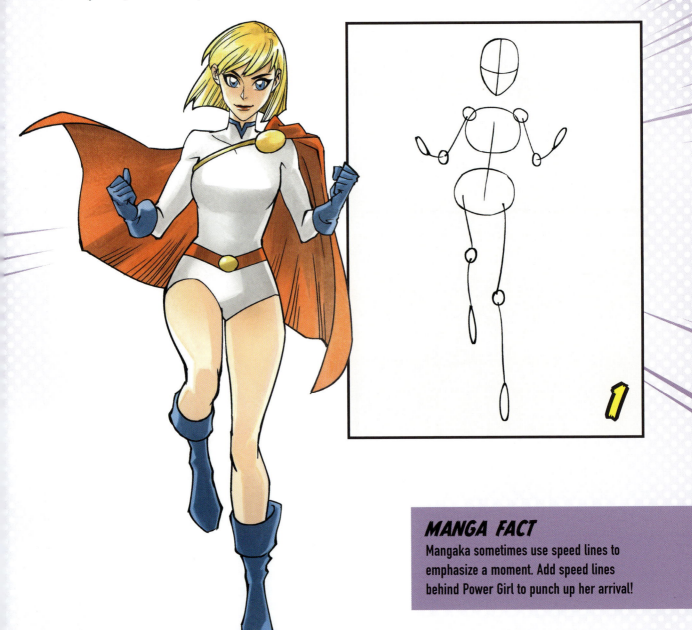

### MANGA FACT

Mangaka sometimes use speed lines to emphasize a moment. Add speed lines behind Power Girl to punch up her arrival!

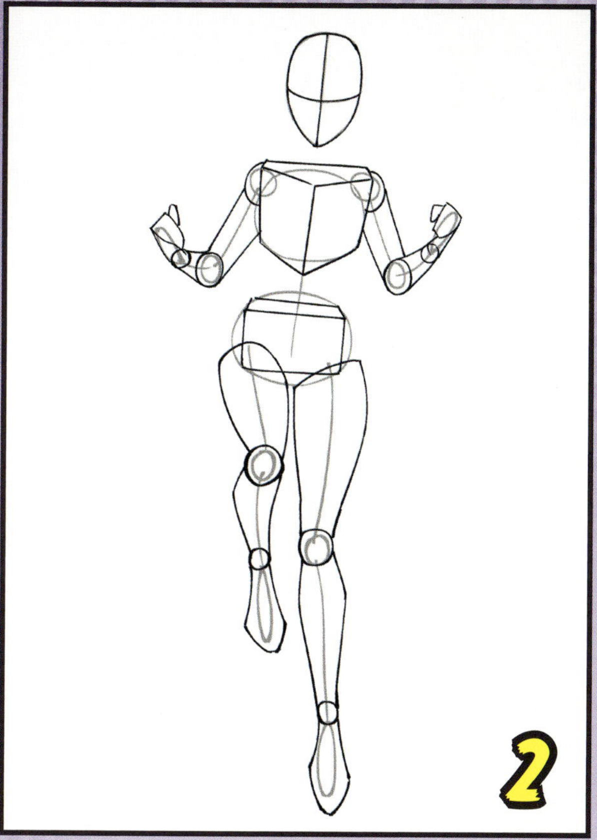
2
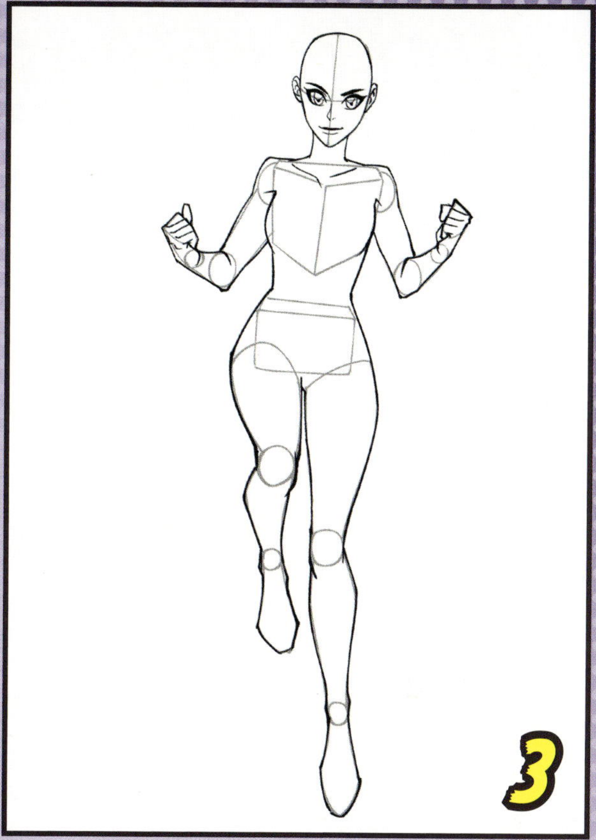
3
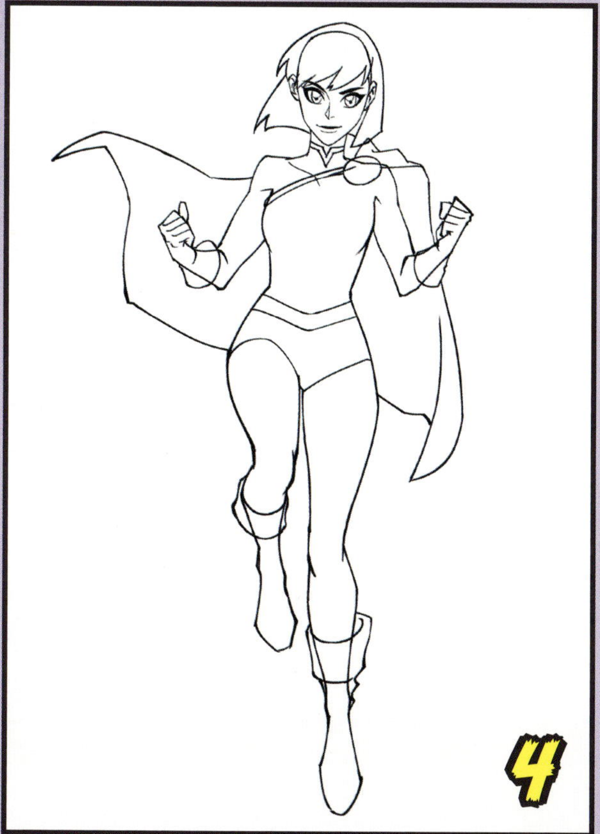
4
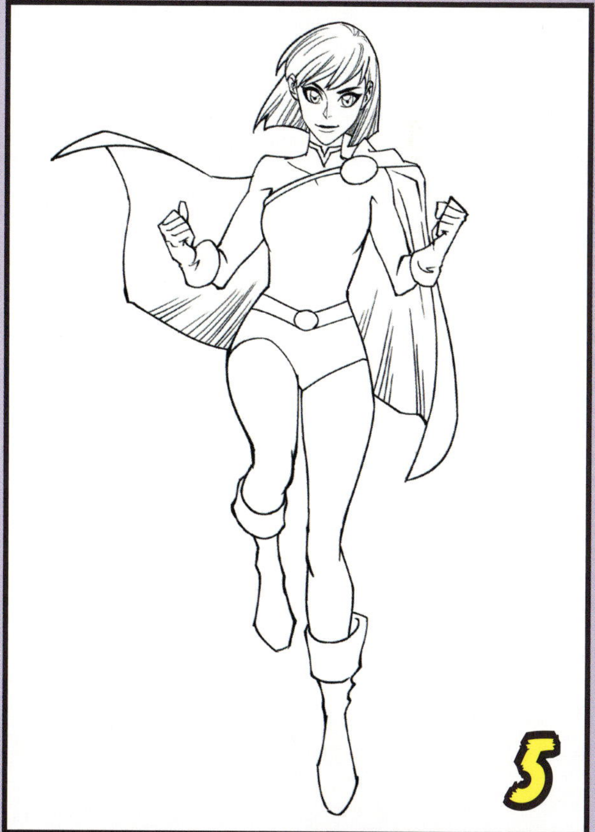
5

# LEX LUTHOR

Lex Luthor's envy is as green as Kryptonite—and just as dangerous. Jealous of Superman's power and popularity, the CEO of LexCorp will stop at nothing to crush the Super Hero. That's why the criminal mastermind often dons his warsuit. Wearing the alien-tech armor, Luthor can pack a wallop to challenge even the Man of Steel!

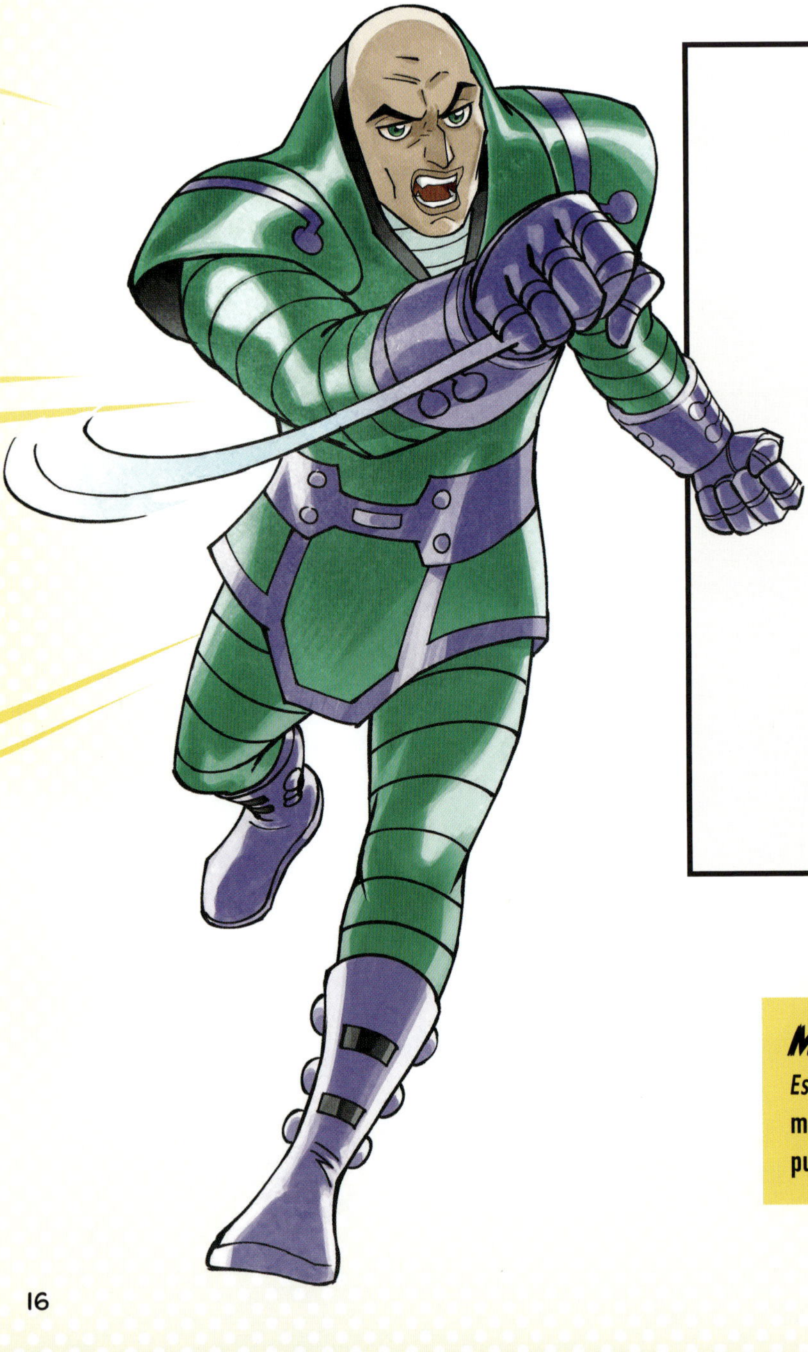

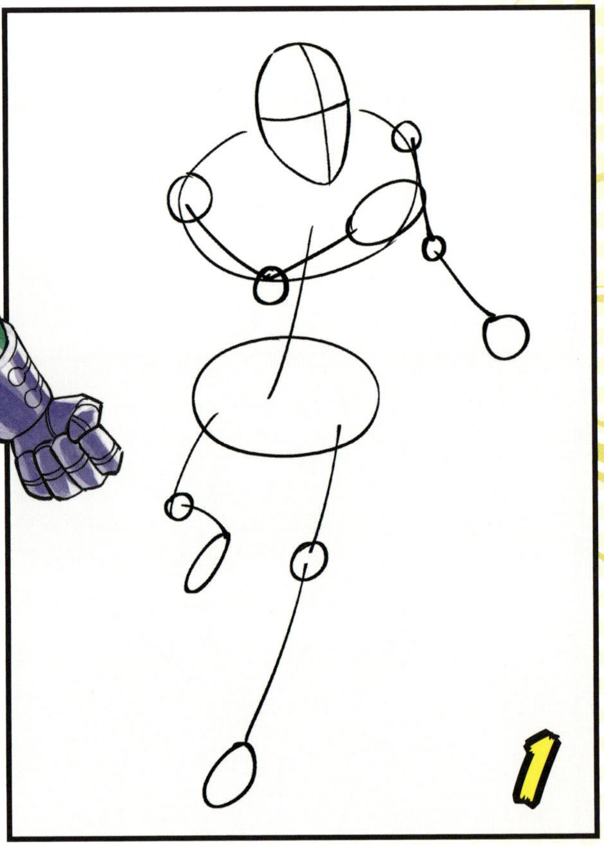
1

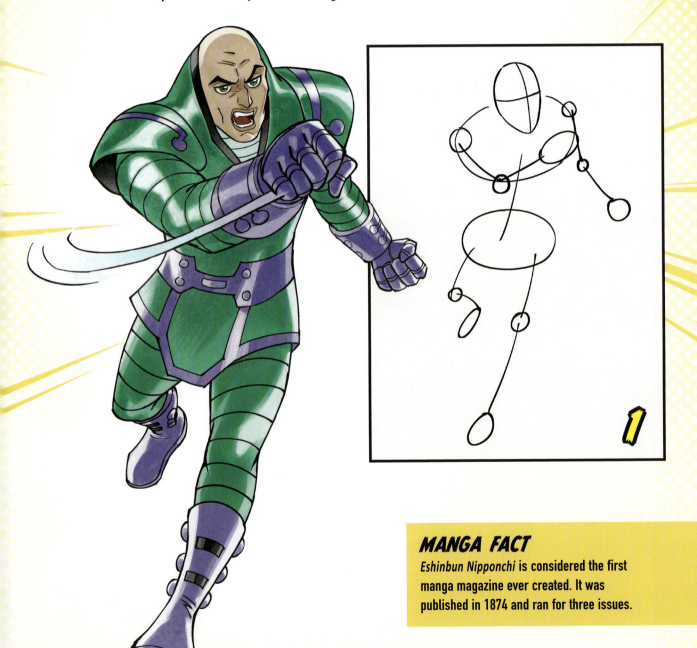

### MANGA FACT

*Eshinbun Nipponchi* is considered the first manga magazine ever created. It was published in 1874 and ran for three issues.

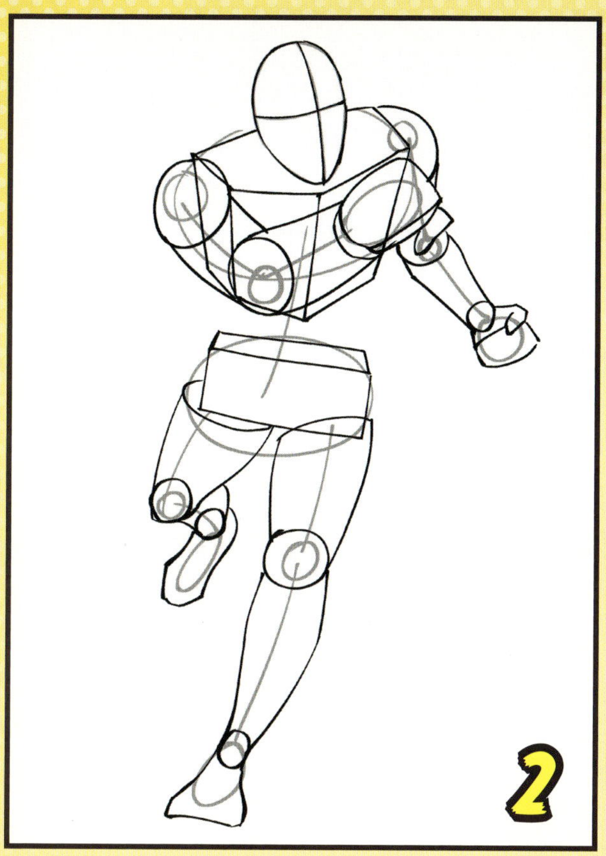
2
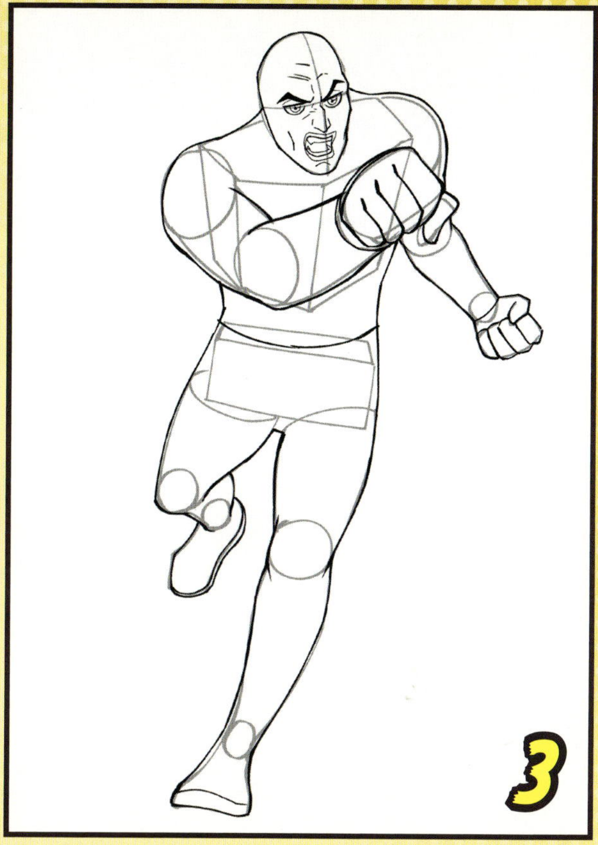
3
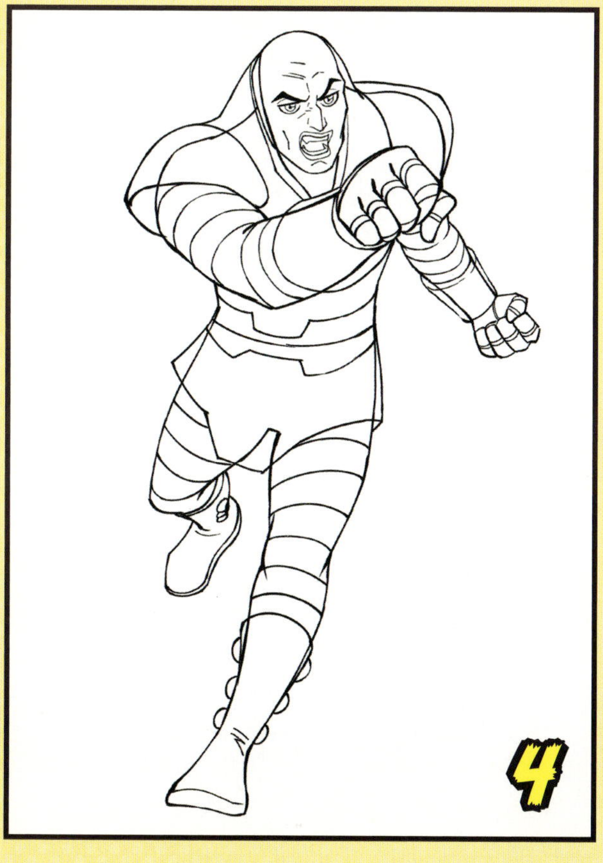
4
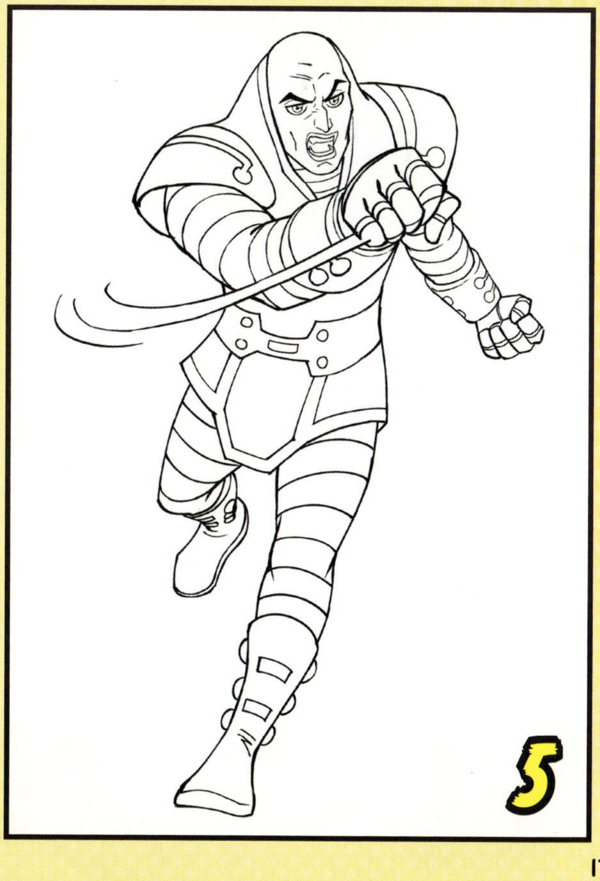
5

# BIZARRO

Is Bizarro a duplicate of doom or an adorable goofball? The jury is still out. This clone of Superman has all the Super Hero's powers, but in reverse. Instead of heat vision and freeze-breath, he unleashes freeze vision and flame-breath. Bizarro's backward heroics often harm more than help. But as he'll tell you, "Bizarro am perfectly imperfect!"

### MANGA FACT
Mangaka use shading to help show mood. Use light shading to play up Bizarro's goofier side. Go heavy for an angry, brooding look.

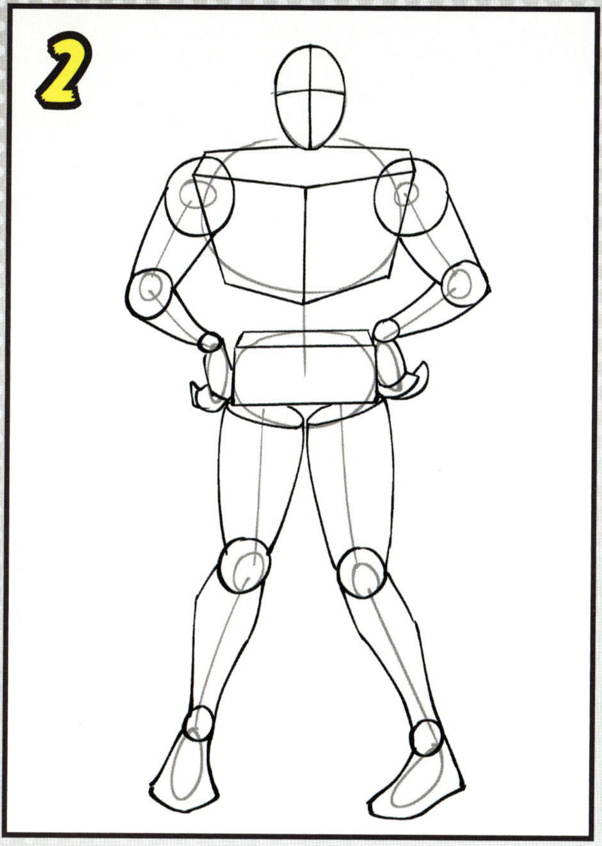
2

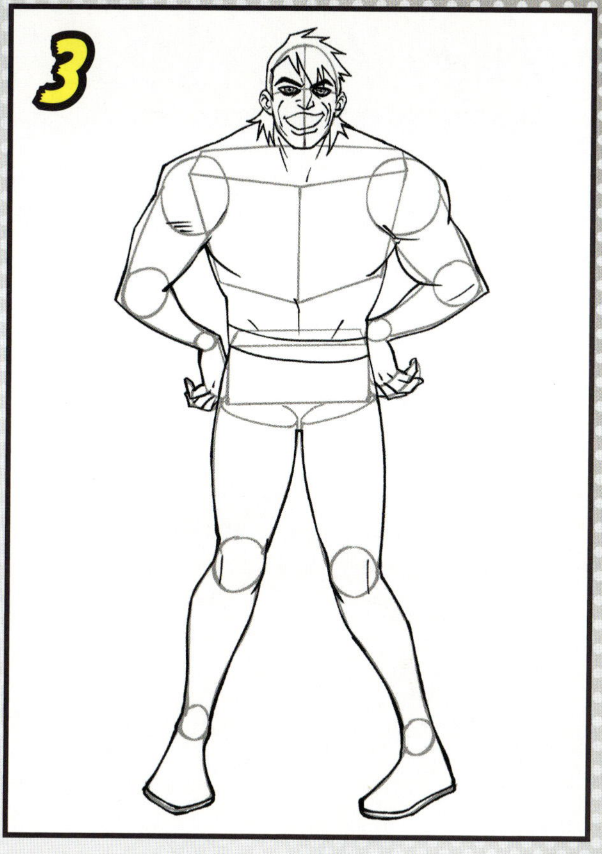
3

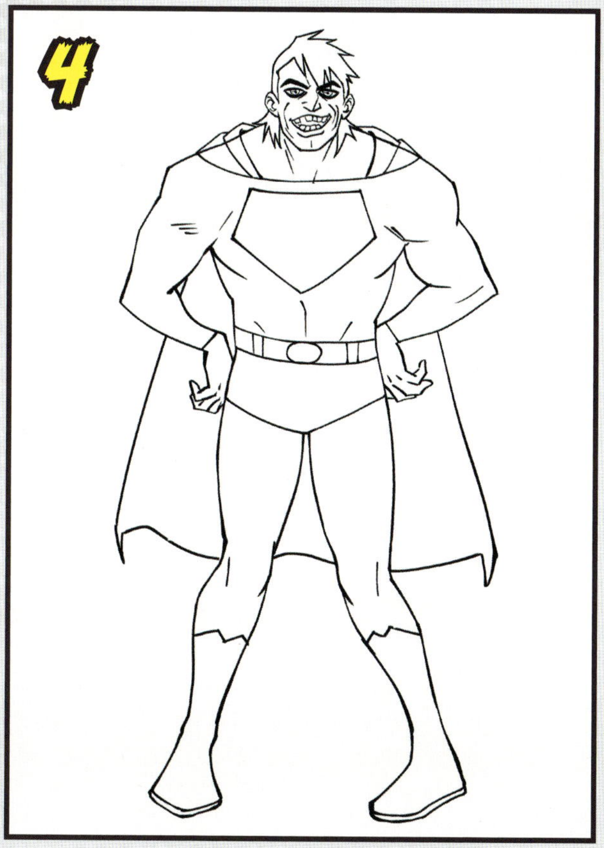
4

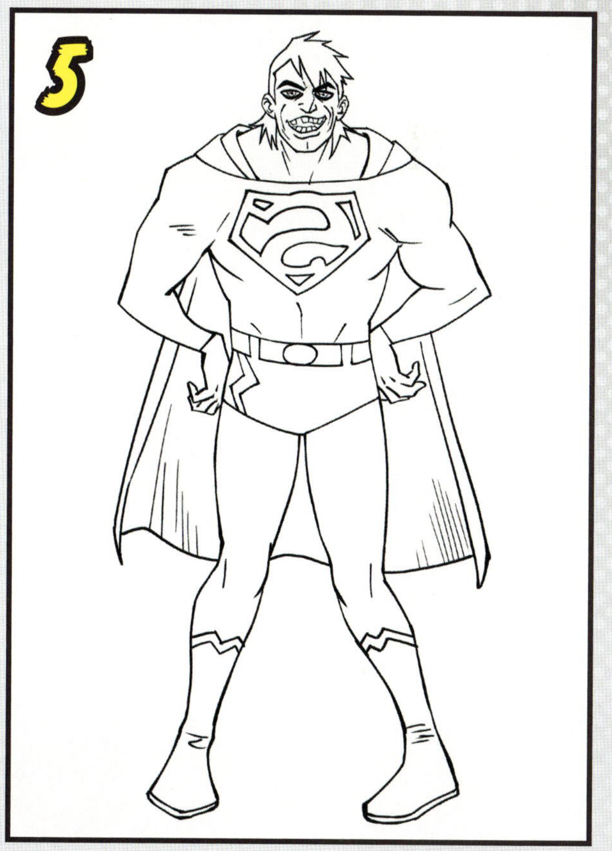
5

# DARKSEID

A word to the wise—don't mess with Darkseid. The ruthless ruler of planet Apokolips is called the God of Tyranny for a reason. His sights are set on conquering the universe! Anyone who dares to defy Darkseid must beware the tyrant's mighty Omega Beams, which can bring even Superman to his knees.

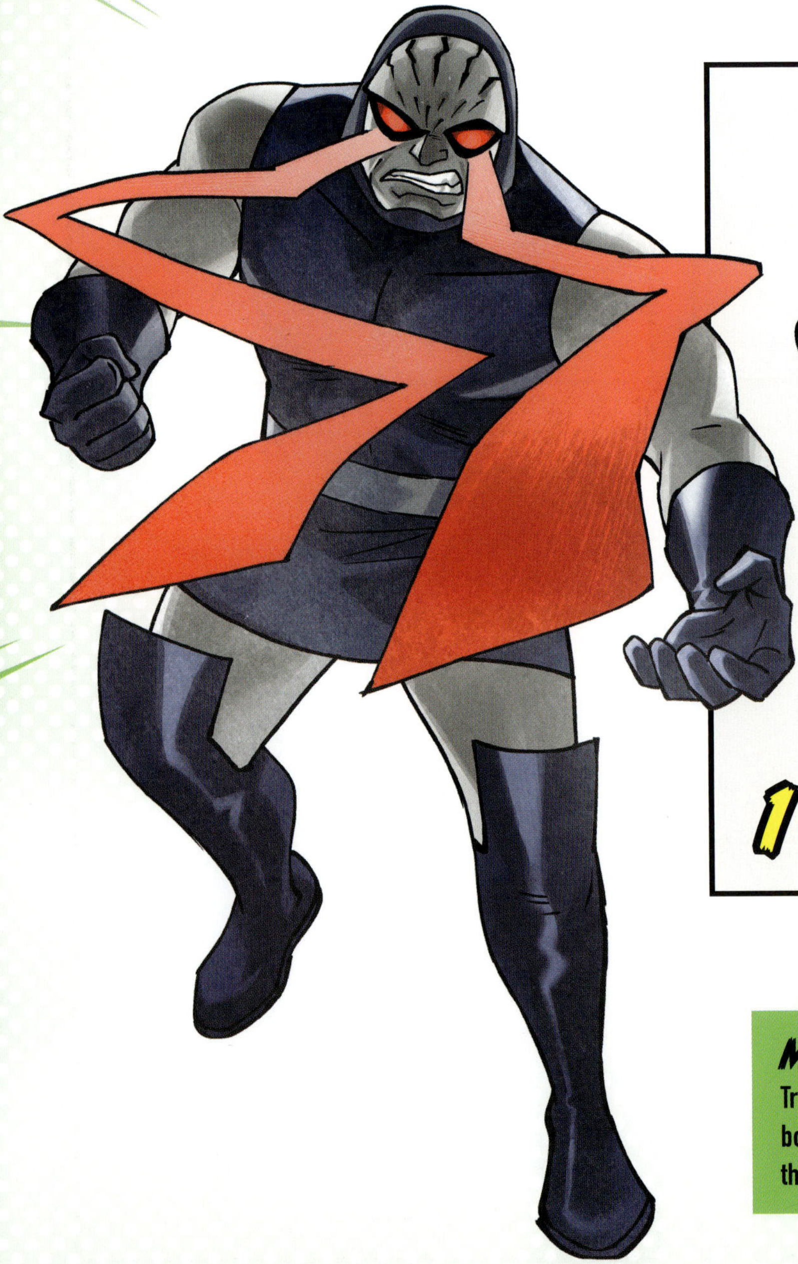

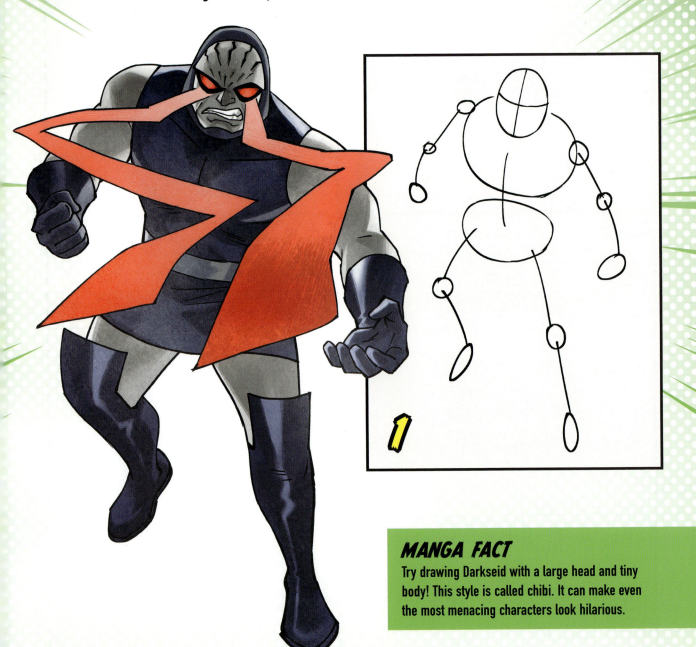

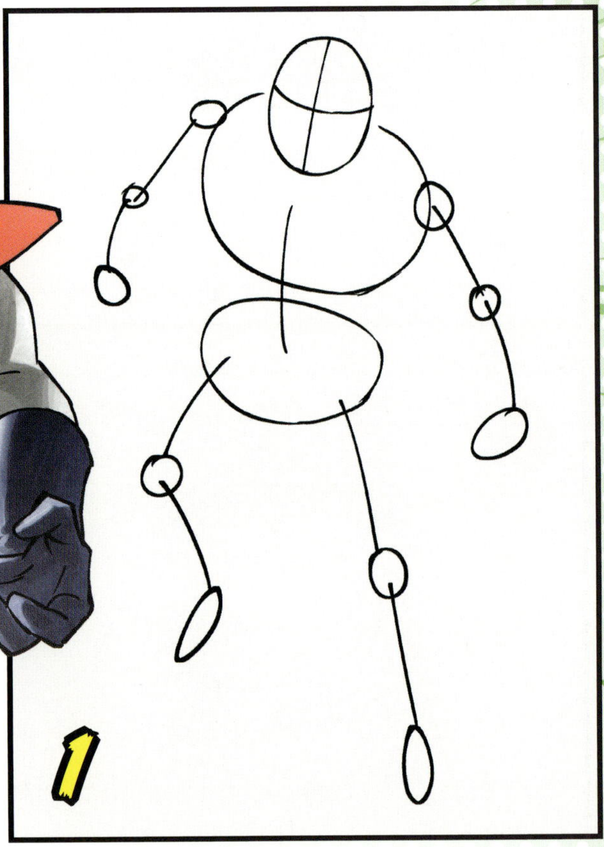
1

### MANGA FACT

Try drawing Darkseid with a large head and tiny body! This style is called chibi. It can make even the most menacing characters look hilarious.

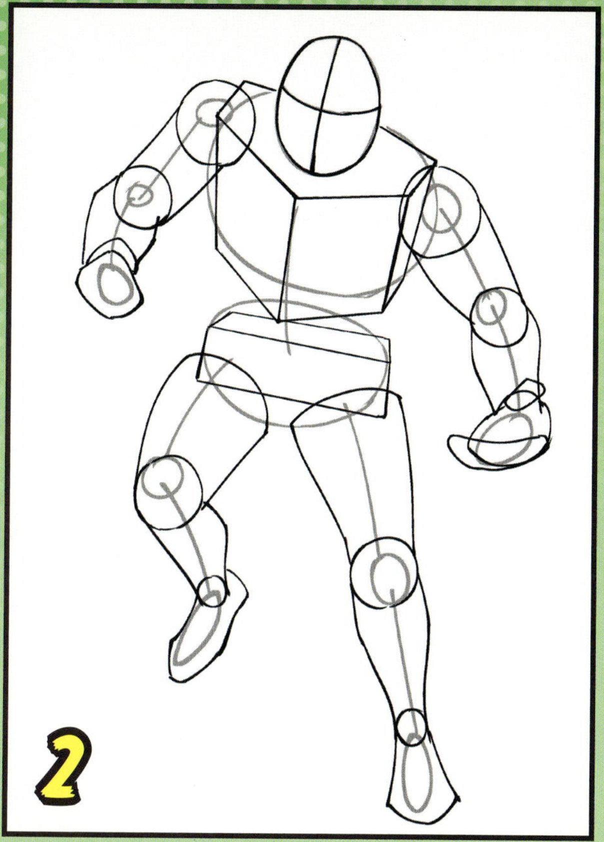
2
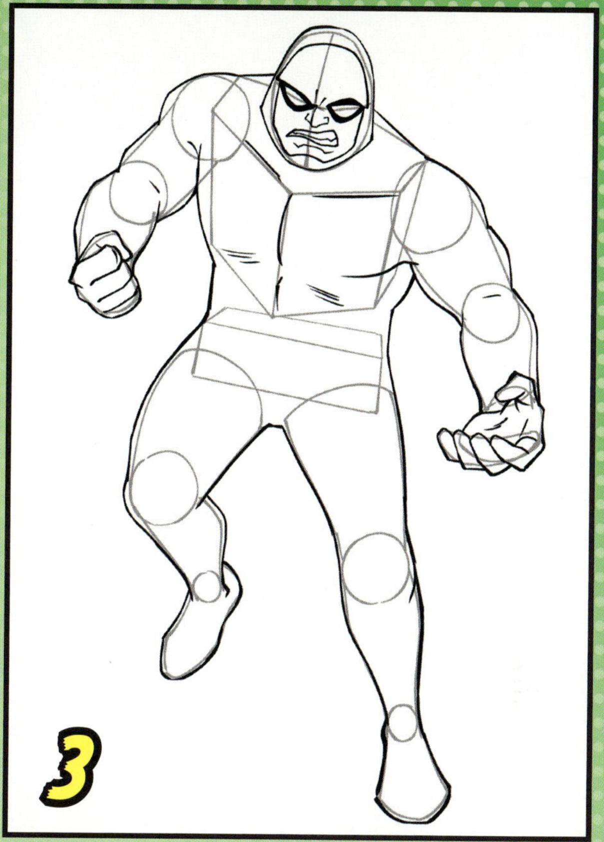
3
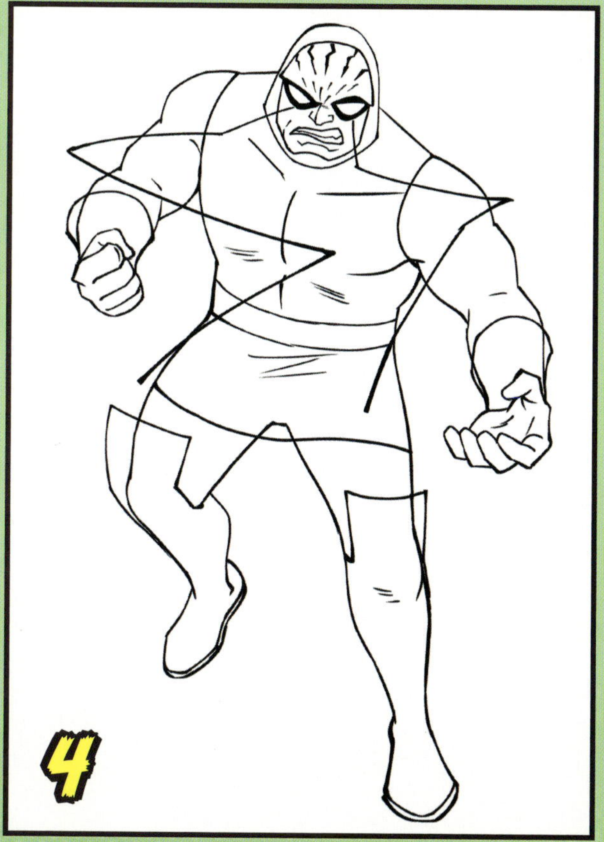
4
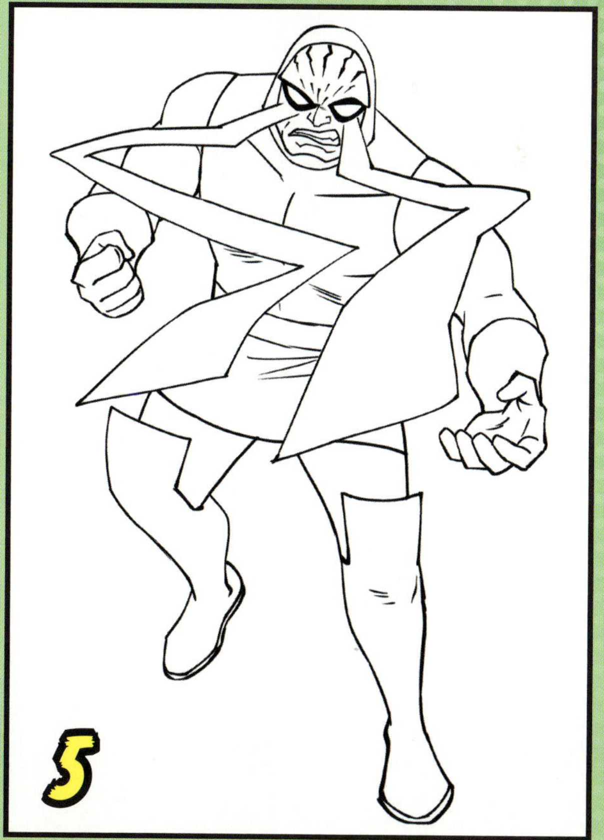
5

# LIVEWIRE

Look out for Livewire! She is positively supercharged with negative energy. The high-voltage Super-Villain can unleash huge amounts of electricity with shocking results. From melting metal to flinging electric energy balls, Livewire has *watt* it takes to conduct mayhem in Metropolis!

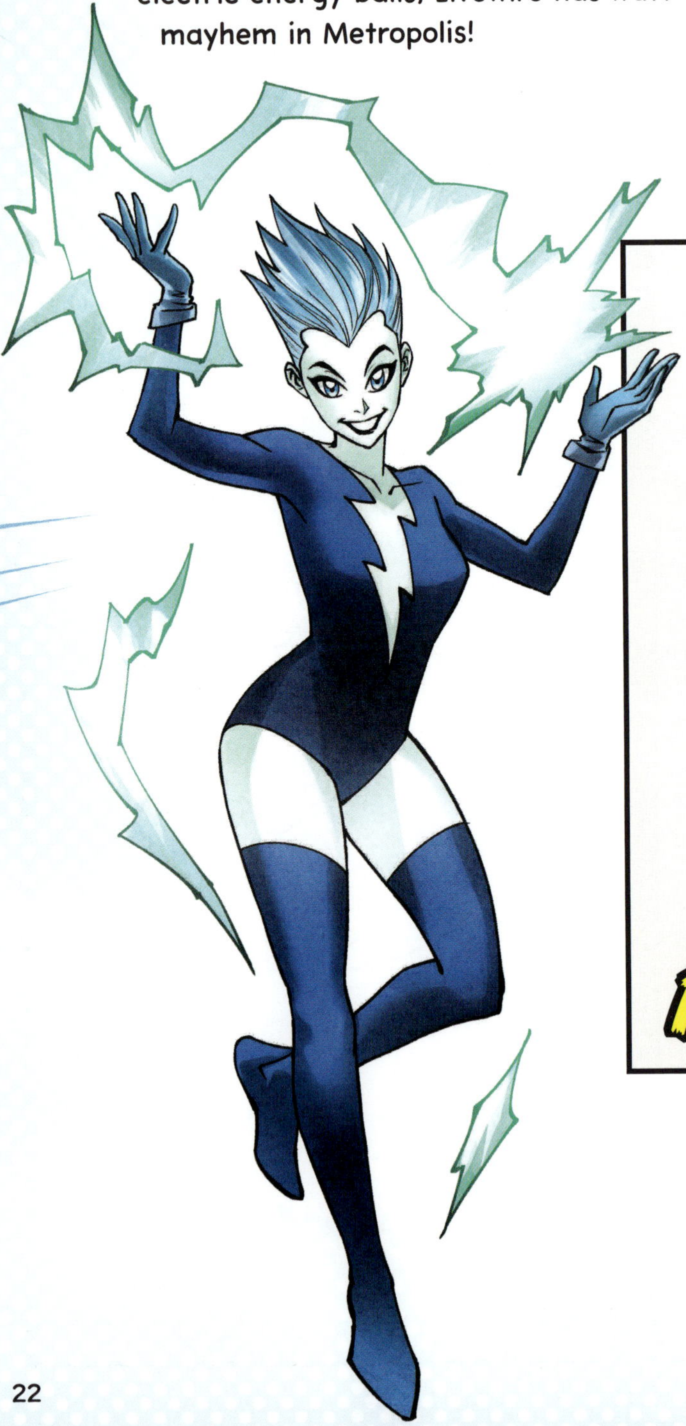

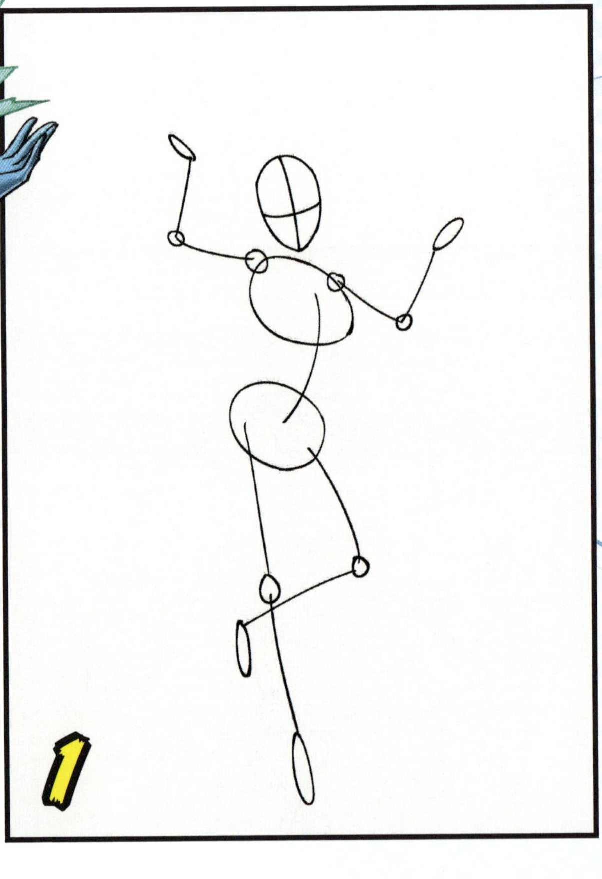

1

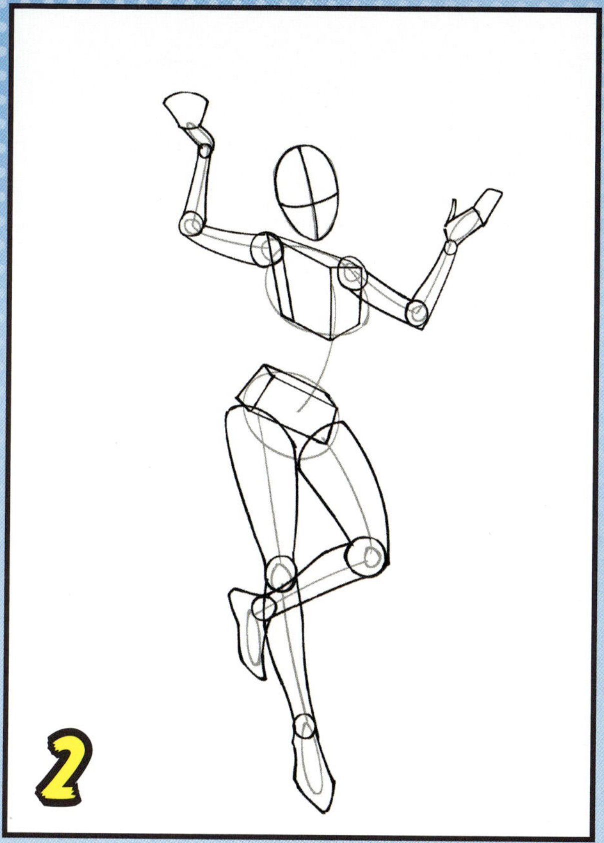
2
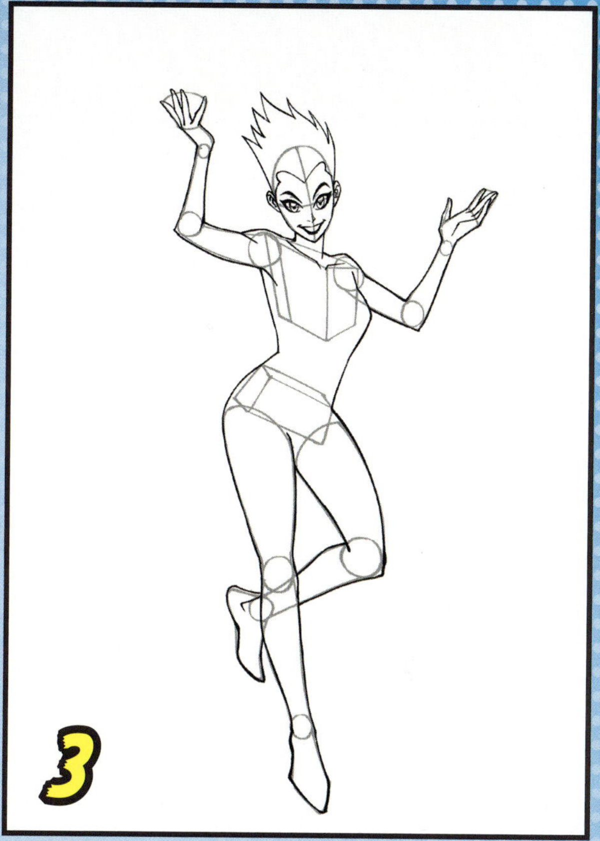
3
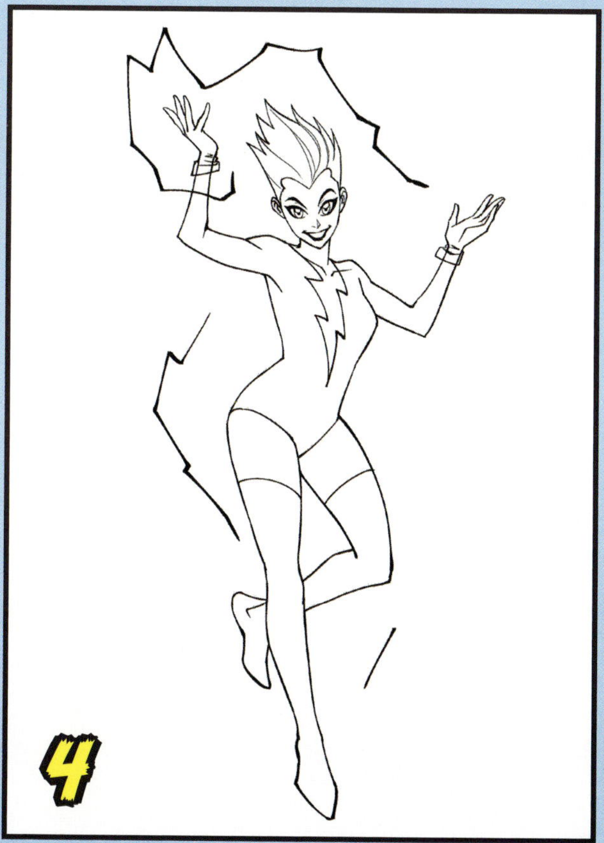
4
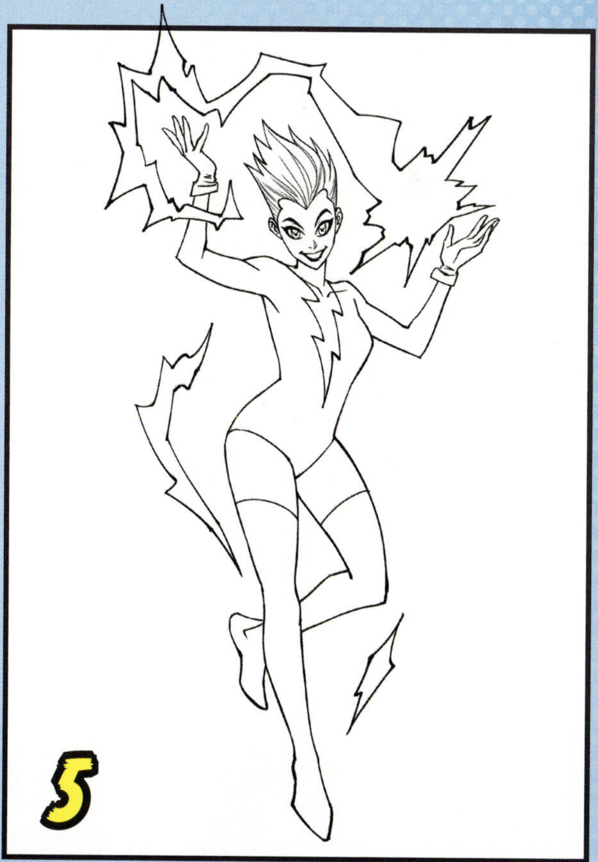
5

# BRAINIAC

For Brainiac, knowledge is power. And this superintelligent supercomputer has a goal that's sinister in its simplicity: Seek out planets, download their raw data, and then destroy them. Naturally, Superman isn't too keen on the evil AI hacking into Earth's databanks with twisting tendrils!

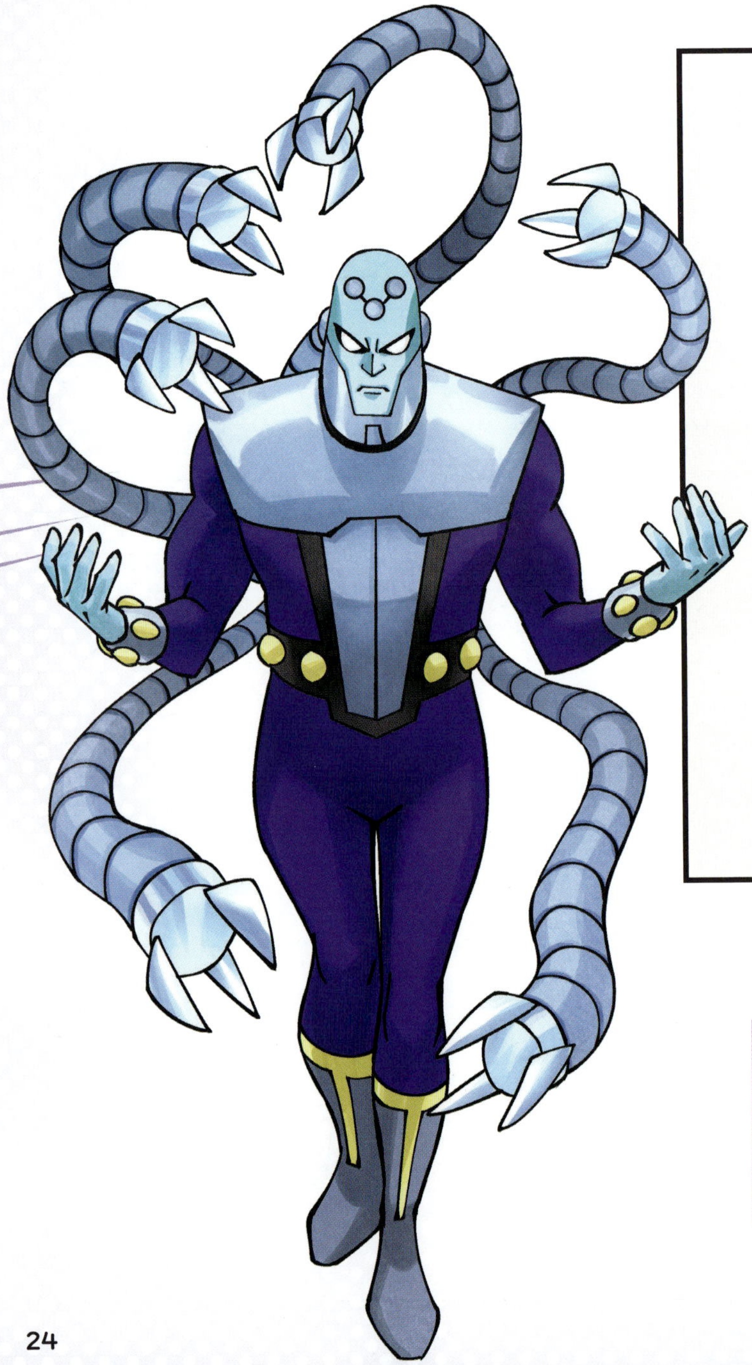

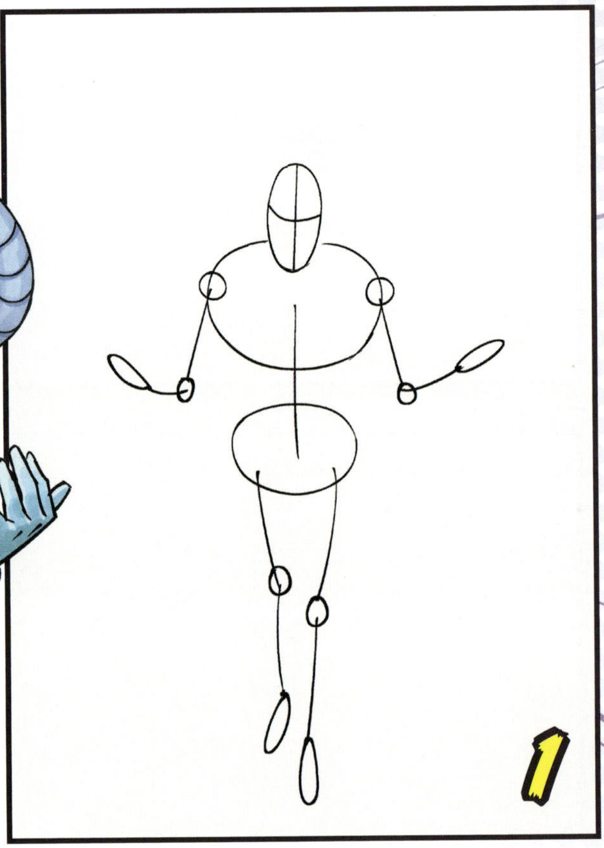
1

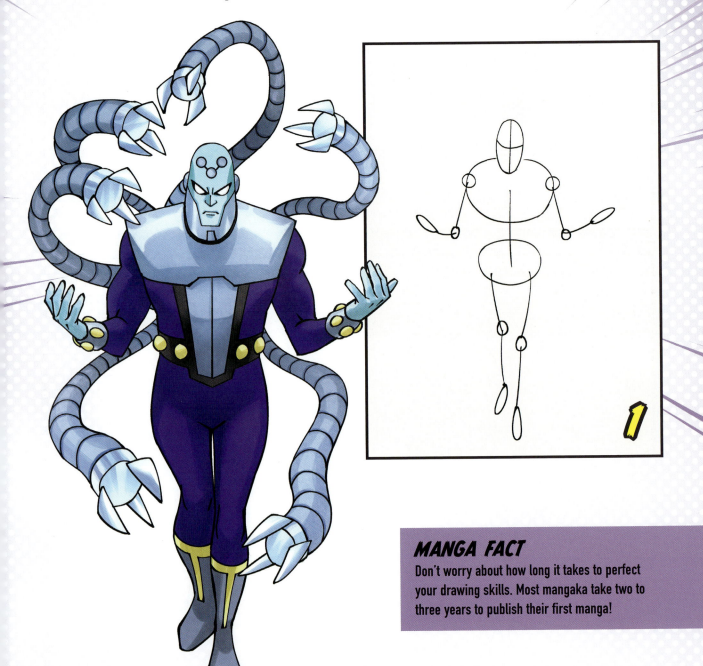

### MANGA FACT

Don't worry about how long it takes to perfect your drawing skills. Most mangaka take two to three years to publish their first manga!

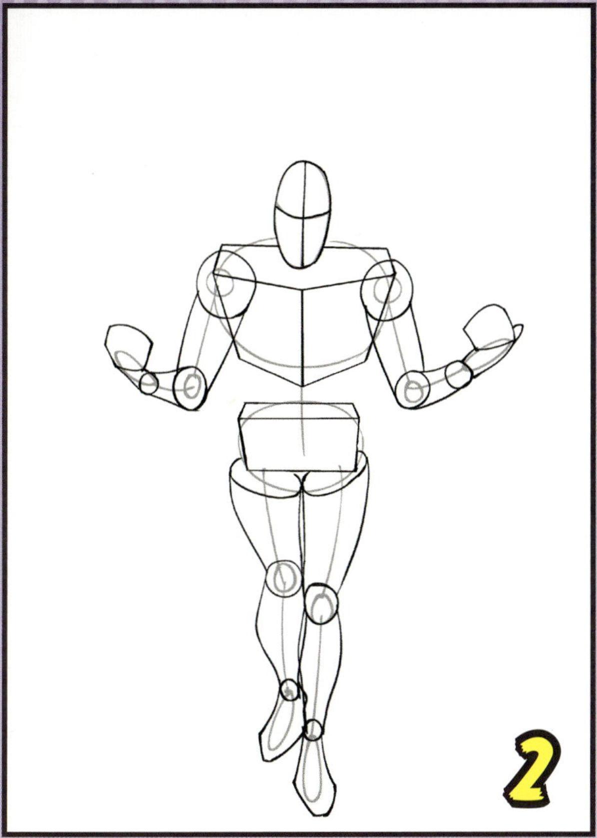
2
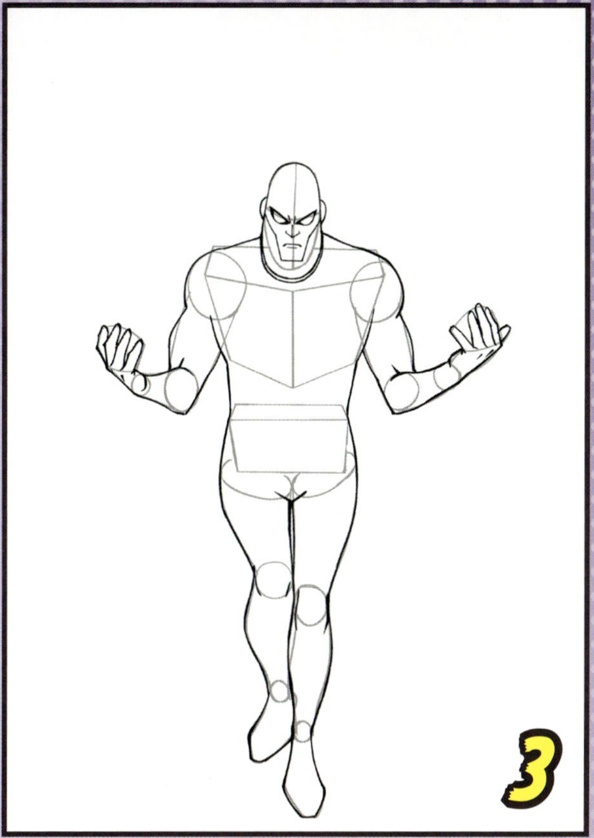
3
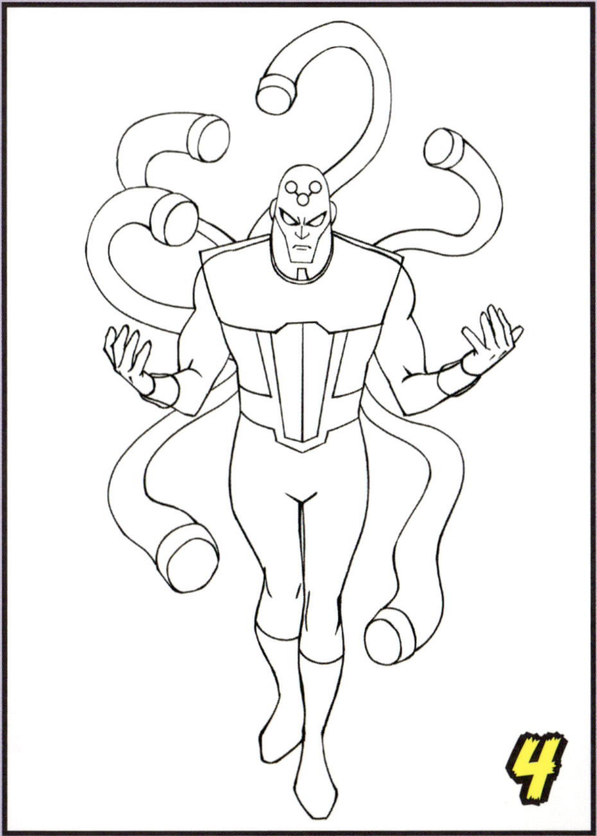
4
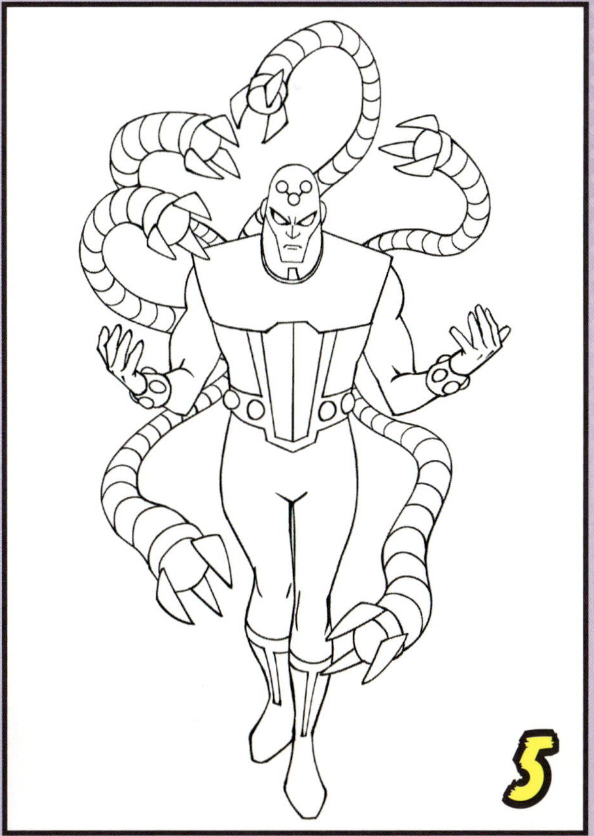
5

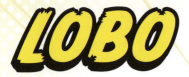

# LOBO

Lobo's word is his bond. When this intergalactic bounty hunter takes a contract, nothing stands in his way. The Main Man—as he's dubbed himself—crisscrosses the galaxy on a souped-up space-bike in pursuit of prey. And when he corners a quarry, he restrains his game with a hook and chain!

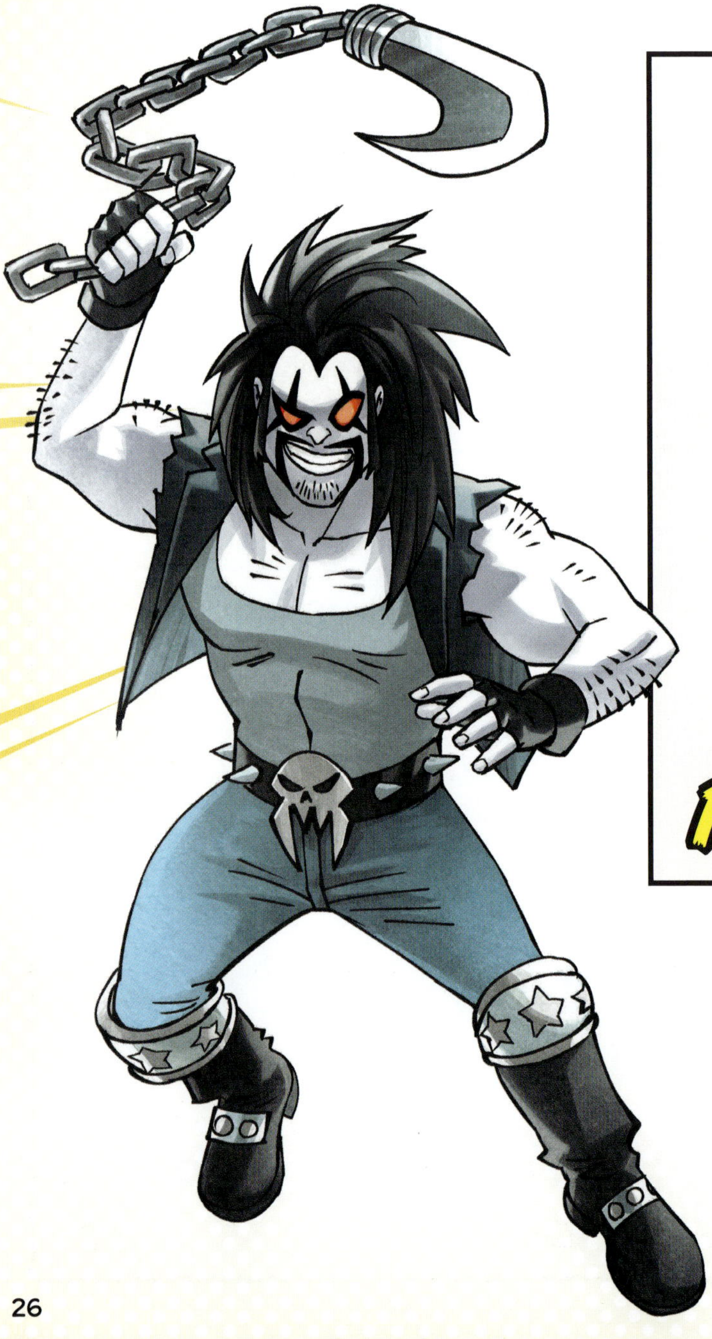

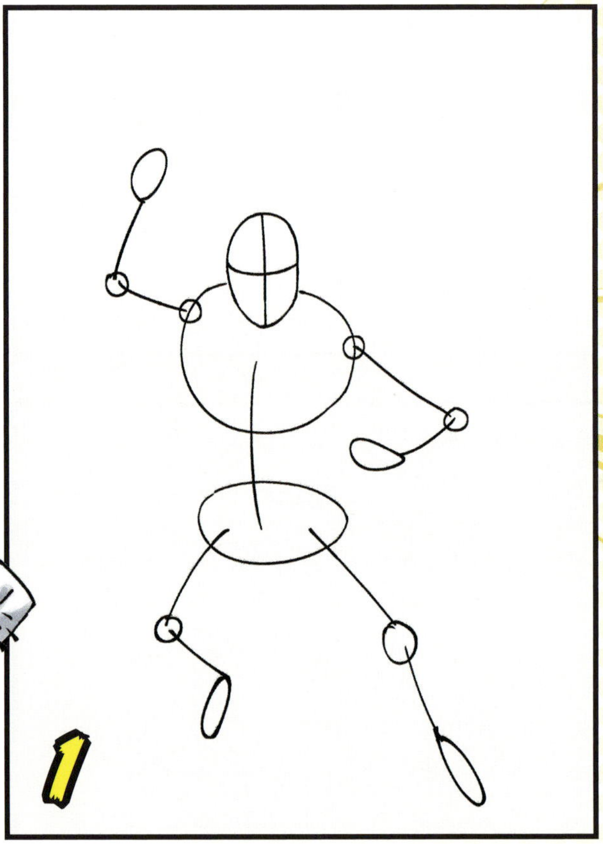
1

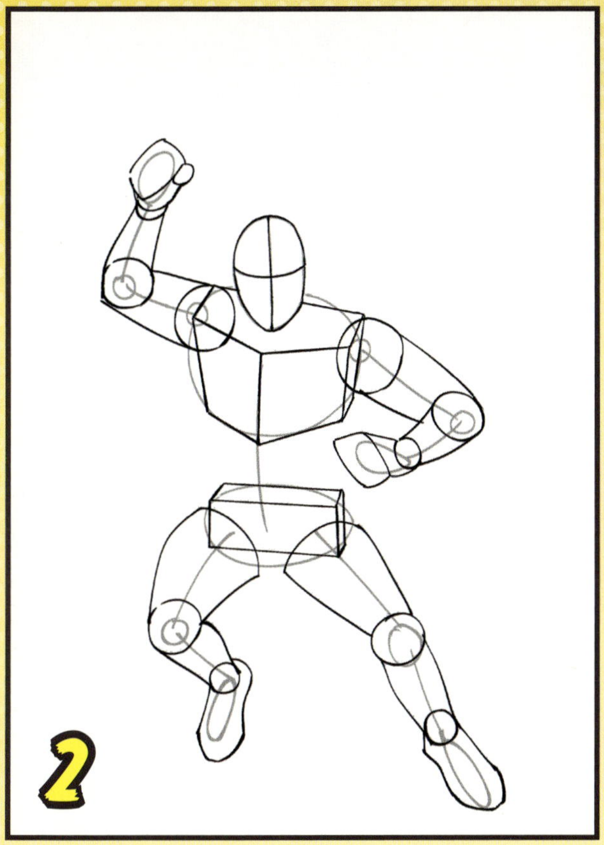
2

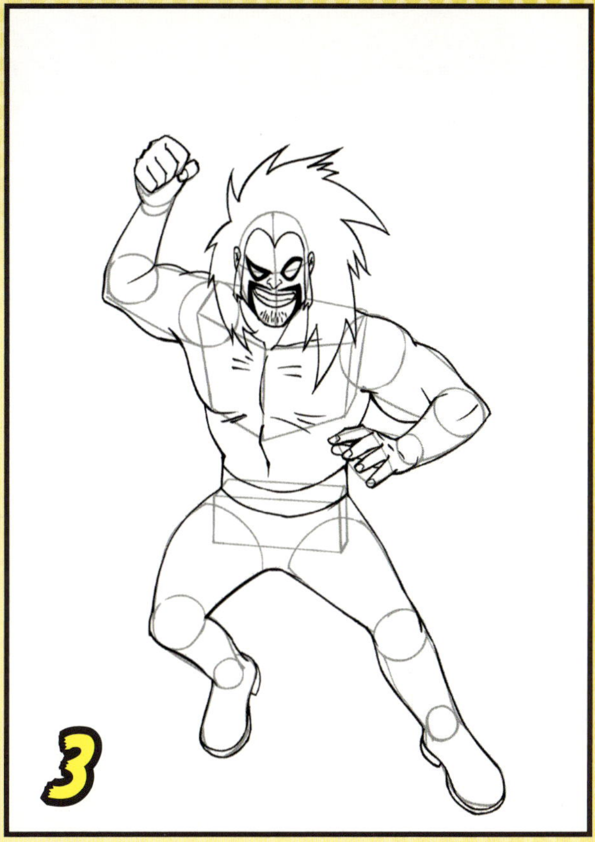
3

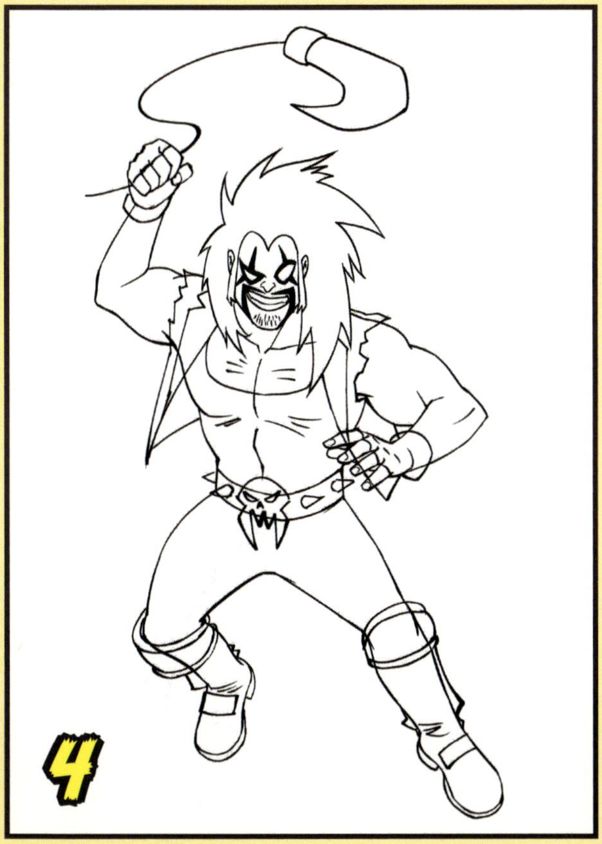
4

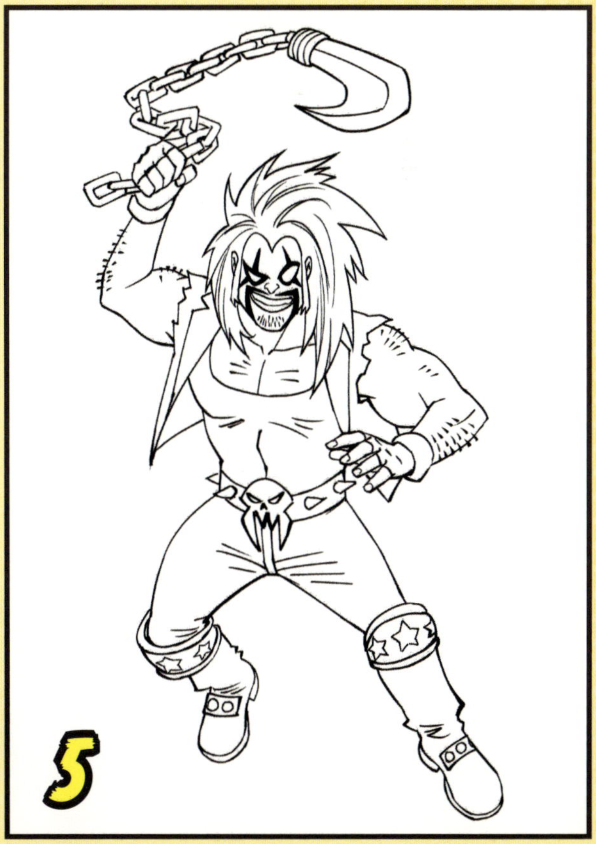
5

# SUPERMAN VS. DOOMSDAY

An epic battle erupts when The World's Greatest Super Hero faces his fiercest foe! Will the dreaded Doomsday release his rage on all of Metropolis? Or can Superman take down the creature of chaos and catastrophe? YOU'RE THE MANGAKA. THE FATE OF THE CITY IS IN YOUR HANDS!

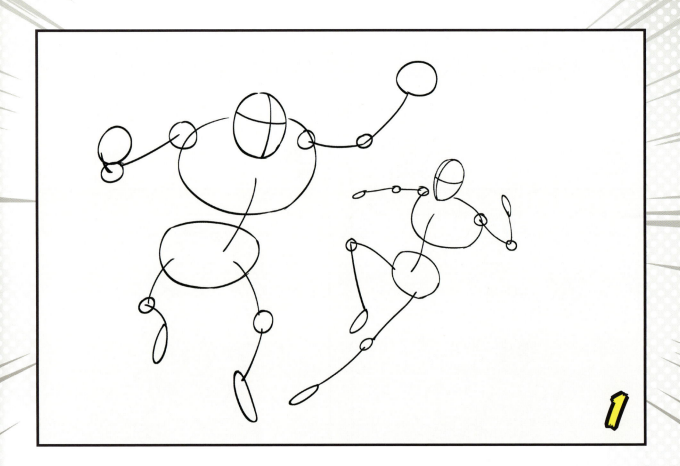

### MANGA FACT
Eiichiro Oda is one of the most successful mangaka of all time. Since 1997, his blockbuster series, *One Piece*, has sold more than 500 million volumes worldwide!

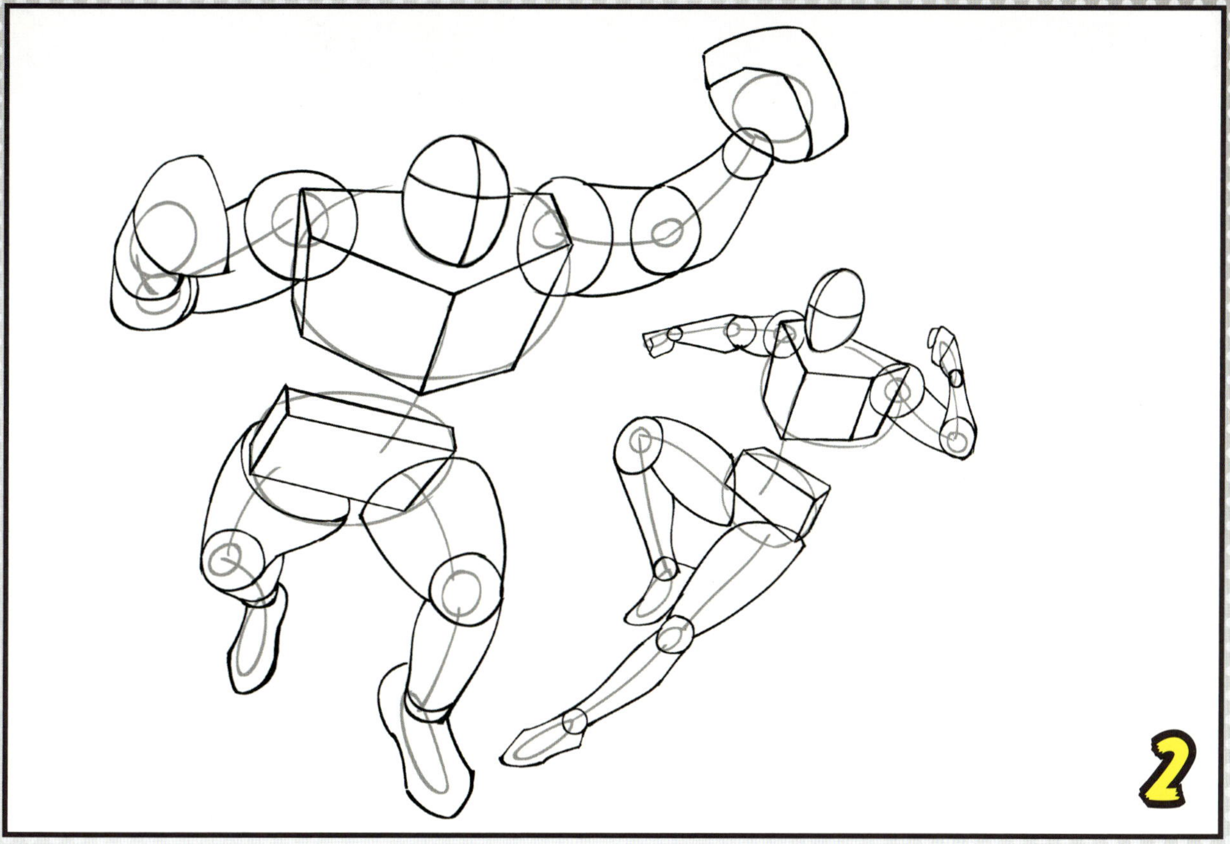
2

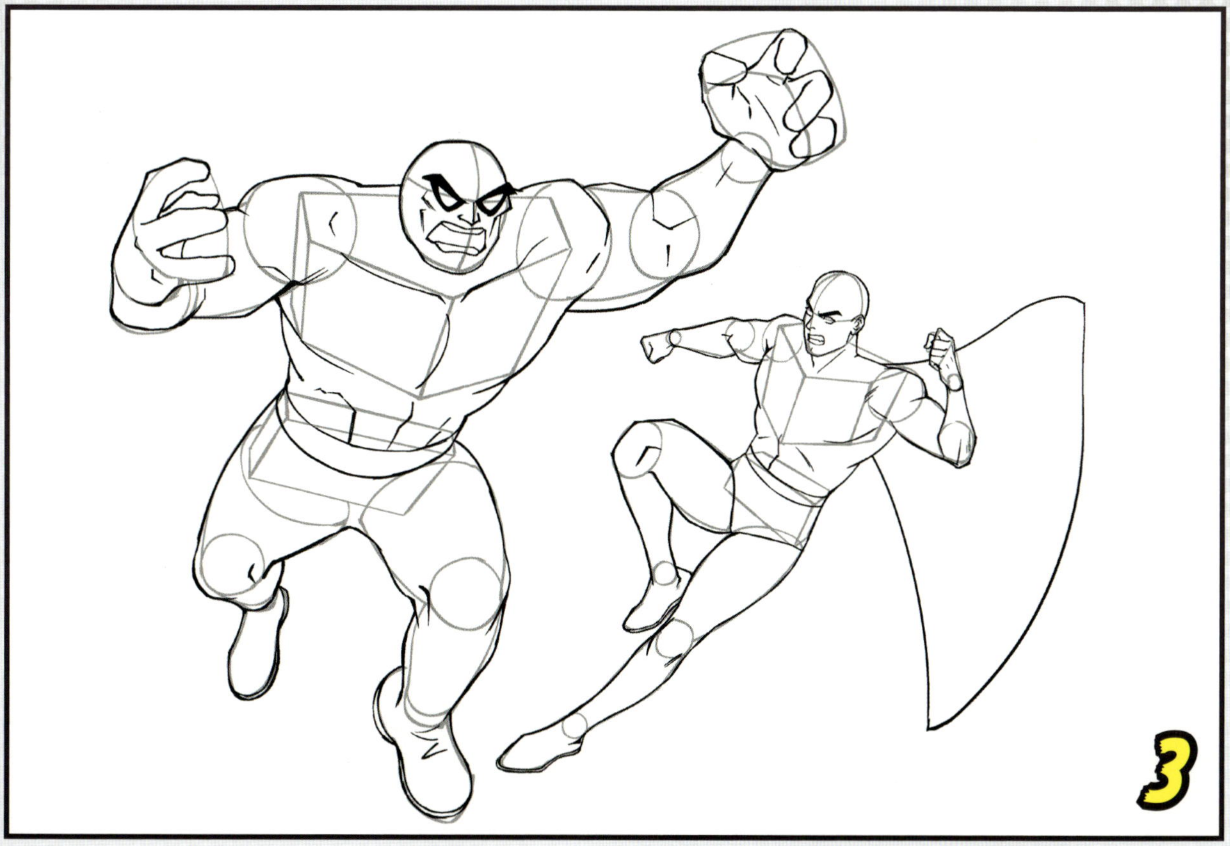
3

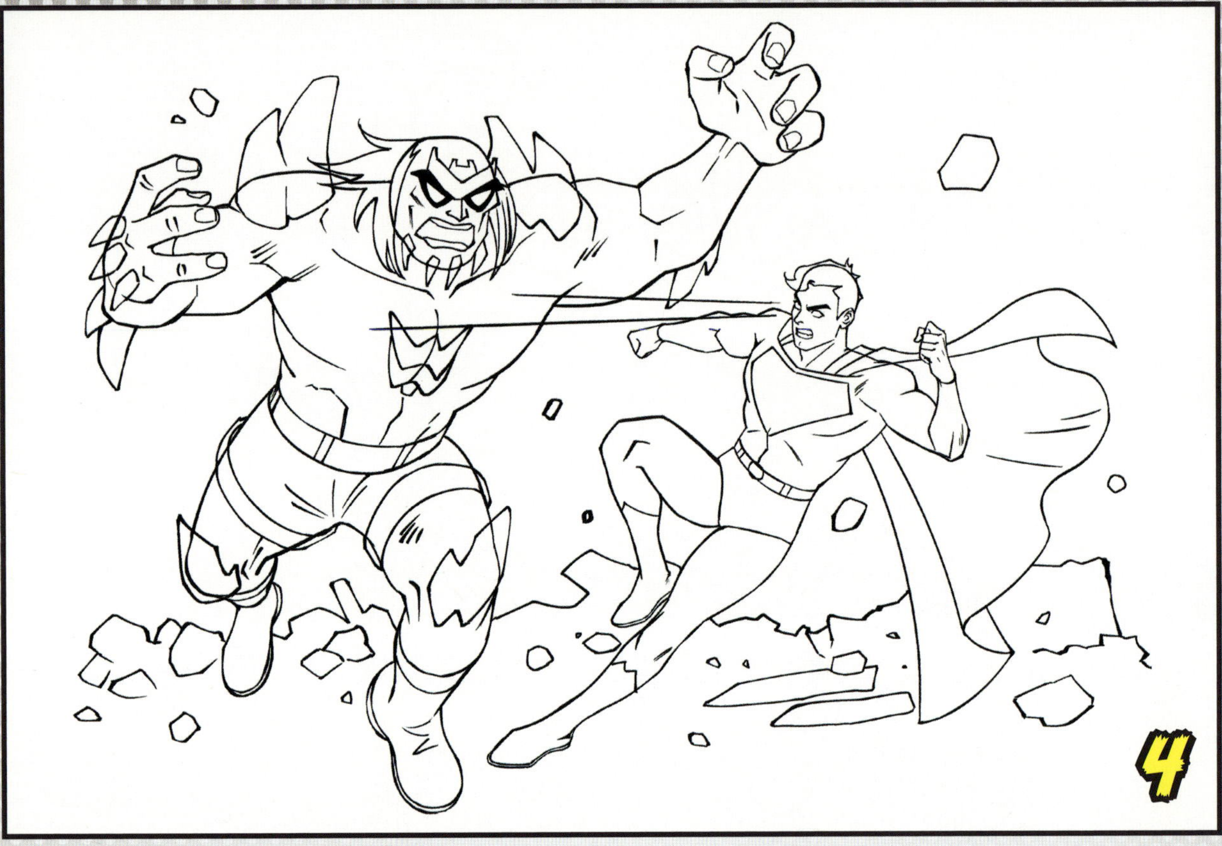
4
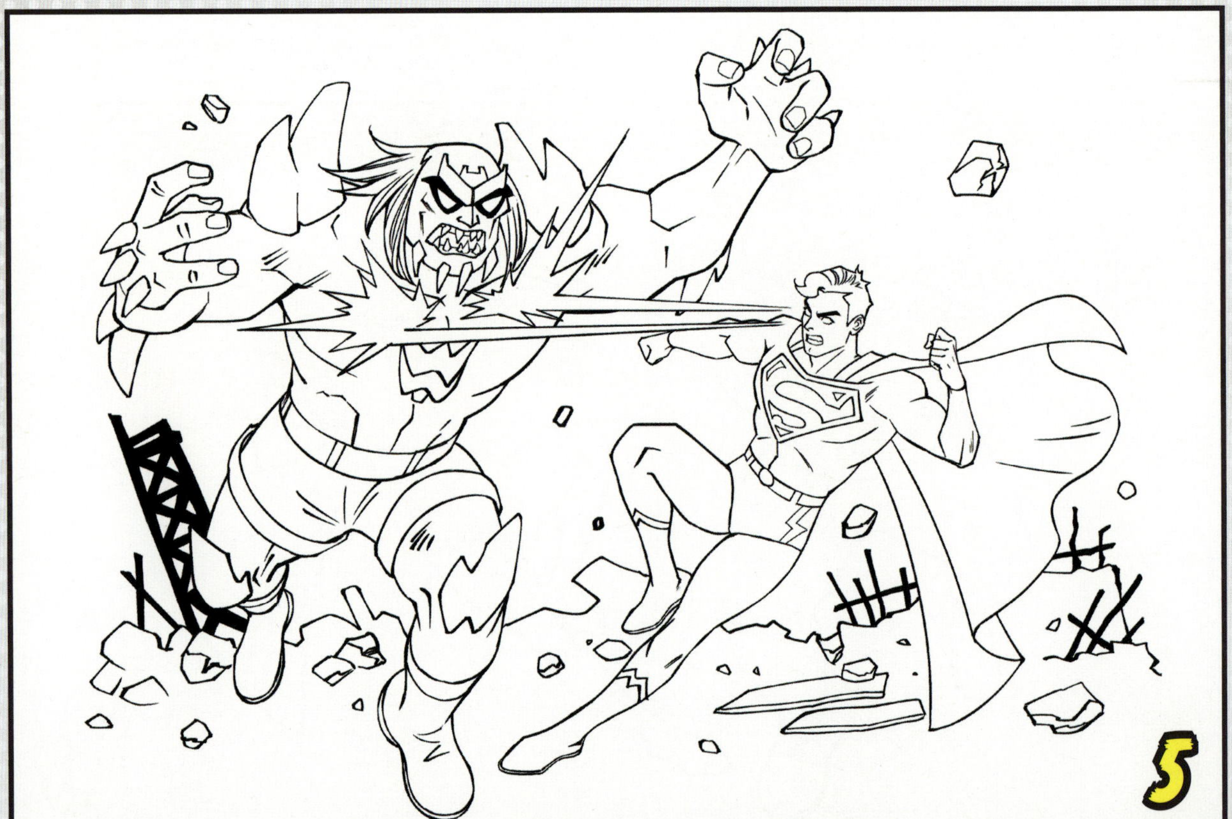
5

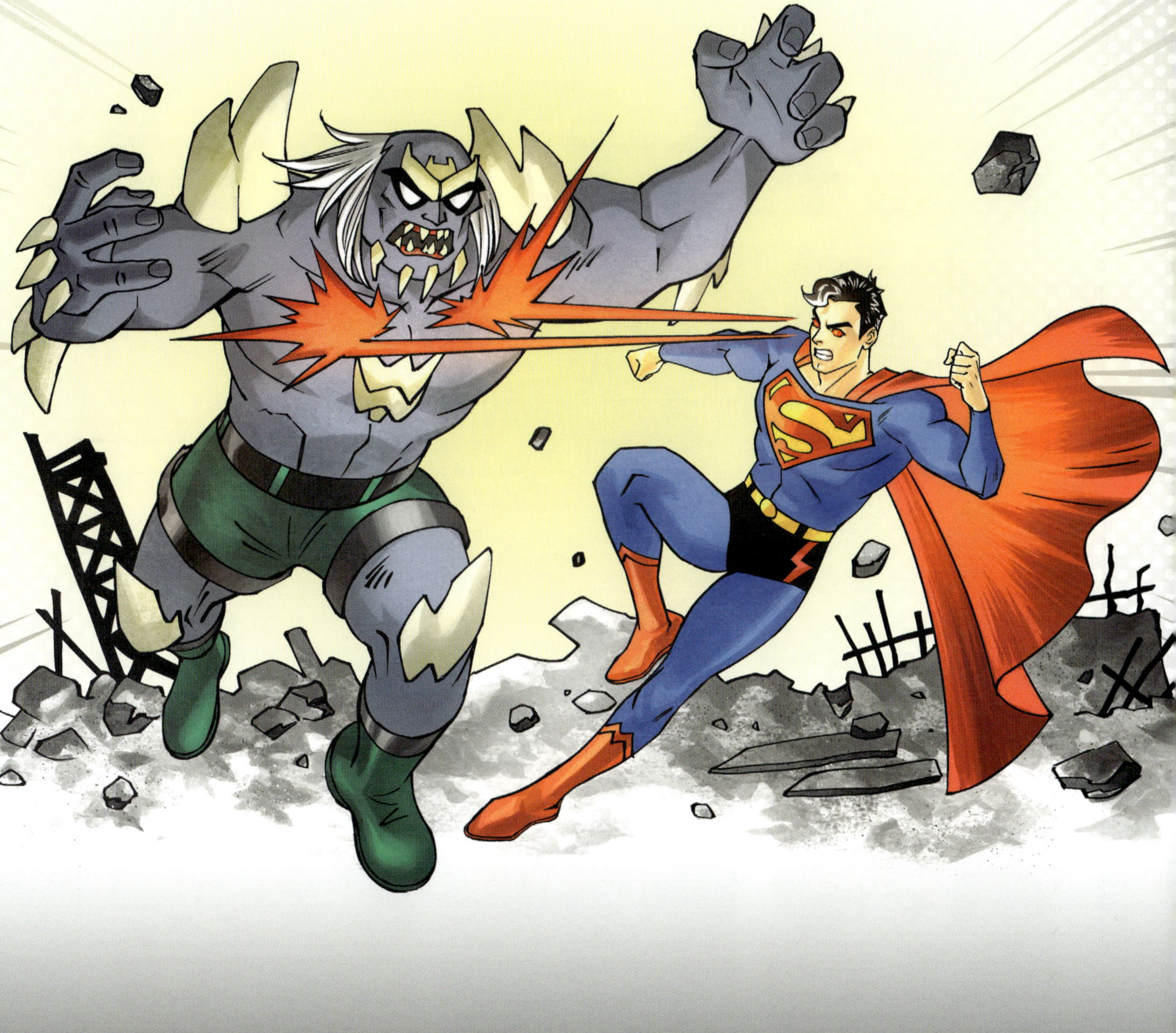

# MORE MANGA DRAWING FUN!


Hart, Christopher. *Drawing Anime from Simple Shapes: Character Design Basics for All Ages.* New York: Drawing with Christopher Hart, 2020.

Whitten, Samantha. *Let's Draw Manga Chibi Characters.* Beverly, MA: Walter Foster Jr., 2023.

Yazawa, Nao. *Drawing and Painting Anime & Manga Faces: Step-by-Step Techniques for Creating Authentic Characters and Expressions.* Beverly, MA: Quarry Books, 2021.


# MORE DC SUPER HERO FUN!

DC
SUPERMAN ORIGAMI
AMAZING FOLDING PROJECTS FEATURING THE MAN OF STEEL
BY JOHN MONTROLL

DC
DC SUPER HEROES
SCHOOL JOKES
BY MICHAEL DAHL & DONALD LEMKE

DC SUPER VILLAINS
LEX LUTHOR
AN ORIGIN STORY

DC
YOU CHOOSE
SUPERMAN
APOKOLIPS INVASION
11 POSSIBLE ENDINGS

DC SUPER HERO ADVENTURES
DC
SUPERMAN
AND THE BIG BOUNTY

DC SUPER HERO ADVENTURES
DC
SUPERGIRL
AND THE MAN OF METAL

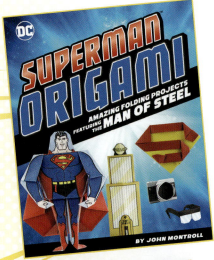

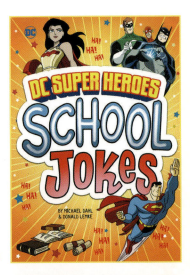

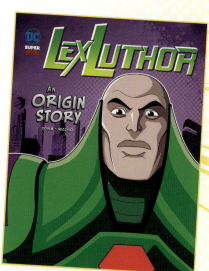

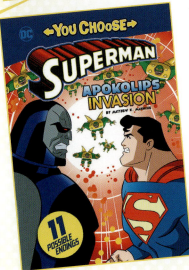

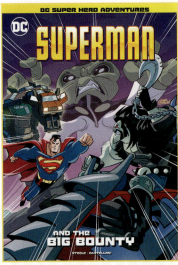

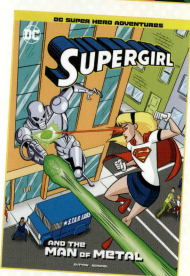